Troubled Mirror

Troubled Mirror

A Study of Yeats's
The Tower

BY DAVID YOUNG

University of Iowa Press
Iowa City

University of Iowa Press, Iowa City 52242
Copyright © 1987 by the University of Iowa
All rights reserved
Printed in the United States of America
First edition, 1987

Book and jacket design by Sandra Strother Hudson
Typesetting by G&S Typesetters, Inc., Austin, Texas
Printing and binding by Edwards Brothers, Inc., Ann Arbor,
Michigan

Library of Congress Cataloging-in-Publication Data

Young, David, 1936–
Troubled mirror.

Includes index.
1. Yeats, W. B. (William Butler), 1865–1939.
Tower. I. Title.
PR5904.T63Y6   1987   821'.8   86-19126
ISBN 0-87745-157-5

Grateful acknowledgment for permission to quote from the
poems of W. B. Yeats is made to the following: A. P. Watt Ltd. on
behalf of Michael B. Yeats and Macmillan London Ltd. for ex-
tracts from *The Collected Poems of W. B. Yeats*; Macmillan Pub-
lishing Co. for a selection from "Fragments," copyright 1933 by
Macmillan, renewed 1961 by Bertha Georgie Yeats; Macmillan
Publishing Co. for extracts from *The Tower*, copyright 1928 by
Macmillan, renewed 1956 by Georgie Yeats.

As we look back over the long gallery of Yeats' major poems, they have more and more the appearance of some series of Renaissance portraits. . . . It is doubtful, therefore, whether they compose an *oeuvre* in the approved literary sense. It is dangerous to mistake their thematic correspondences and linking symbols for a unity which is lacking: for that is to confuse the ideology and the biography with the works of art which are born from them. There is a sense in which the completest collection of Yeats' poems is still an anthology. After *The Wanderings of Oisin*, Yeats never wrote another "long poem," and it is no use pretending that what we have constitutes one.

Peter Ure, *W. B. Yeats*

It gets more and more deliberate as one examines it. . . . Through that volume, *The Tower*, runs a dramatic progression if ever I saw one. And the presence of such a progression, once it is discerned, modifies all the parts.

Hugh Kenner, "The Sacred Book of Arts," in *Gnomon*

Contents

Preface *ix*

1. Affinities and Juxtapositions   *1*

2. Byzantium and Back   *14*

3. Empty Houses   *30*

4. A Requiem for Progress   *46*

5. Fabulous Darkness   *61*

6. Swan and Centaur   *73*

7. The Long Schoolroom   *85*

8. Sophocles in Ireland   *97*

9. The Death of the Hare   *107*

10. Muscatel in Oxford   *120*

11. A Bitter Book   *134*

Notes   *145*

Index   *151*

Preface

While not many readers would dispute the claim that Yeats is the greatest modern poet in our language, the basis of that claim is surprisingly difficult to identify. We are still very much in the process of describing and understanding both the greatness and the modernity of this poet. If by greatness we mean an achievement that ranks Yeats with poets like Chaucer, Spenser, Milton, and Wordsworth, we must acknowledge that those poets' claims to greatness rest in large part on ambitious long poems like *The Faerie Queene* and *The Prelude*. While Yeats tried his hand at a long poem (*The Wanderings of Oisin*), his achievement clearly rests on individual lyrics of intensity, scope, and memorability. The creation of such lyrics, at least as tradition has it, does not guarantee greatness. No long poems, the formula runs, no major poet.

The question of Yeats's modernism is at least as problematic. Much of the existing commentary ignores the question. Yeats is variously presented as a romantic poet who happened to survive into the twentieth century, as an Irishman who wrote poetry in a kind of Celtic twilight, and as an occultist and visionary whose preoccupations somehow put him beyond the periods, movements, and other cultural entanglements most poets experience. That he has strong similarities to other great modernists like Stravinsky and Picasso is by no means clear.

I propose in this study to shed light on both questions through a careful account of Yeats's greatest volume of poems, *The Tower* (1928). It is not simply that the book represents Yeats at his best and his most modern, but that a book of poems is, for this poet, the deliberate equivalent of the long poems of tradition. The order of the poems in *The Tower* is a careful design, and they were written, revised, and arranged in such a way as to make a whole that is both dramatically and thematically greater than the sum of its parts.

There is only one way to demonstrate the claim that *The Tower's* greatness rests on the careful ordering of individual lyrics to make up an equivalent to a traditional long poem, and that is by tracing its progression, poem by poem, to show how the ordering works. This enterprise requires close readings of individual poems, and while such attention might threaten to duplicate existing criticism, we come here upon another curious fact about Yeats's putative greatness: that many of his finest or most interesting poems remain largely unexplicated. The reader who looks for satisfactory accounts of such well-known poems as "Among School Children" and "Leda and the Swan" will probably be disappointed, at least in getting answers to some of the most difficult questions these poems raise, and the reader in search of help with more obscure poems such as "On a Picture of a Black Centaur by Edmund Dulac" or "Two Songs from a Play" will be even more frustrated. Close readings of some of Yeats's finest and most difficult poems will turn out to be a useful byproduct of this attempt to explain the interdependence of his greatness and his modernism.

The term "close reading" invokes the currently unfashionable critical approach known as New Criticism. While I confess here to some affinities with that school, I must point out that one of the major assumptions of New Criticism, that of the independence of the individual lyric, is probably what prevented the approach to Yeats that I have undertaken here. If one assumes that a complete reading of, say, "Sailing to Byzantium" can be produced without reference to anything else, then it does not matter that that poem is first in *The Tower* and that it is immediately followed by "The Tower," which promptly falls back into the "problem," old age, that "Sailing" appeared to have resolved. My contention is that the best way to read Yeats's lyrics is through attention to the context he created for them: it is not their independence but their lack of it, their *interdependence*, that I wish to stress.

Actually, I can claim to be critically up-to-date in a number of ways. I shall be exploring "intertextuality" in *The Tower*, though that term is usually reserved for significant relations that develop among literary texts by different authors rather than by the same one. I shall also be doing some "deconstructing" of literary texts, as just now, when I claimed that the apparent "solution" of "Sailing to Byzantium" breaks down and leaves that poem imperfect and, in a sense, incomplete. But my primary methodology is dictated not by my theoretical affinities but simply by Yeats's practice. He saw— quite possibly through his work in the theater—that major literary forms could thrive on opposing viewpoints and contrary possibilities, and that fragments of experience and facets of emotional response could be juxtaposed with little interpretive emphasis to release meaning and build cumulative experiences of great power. The further he pursued these insights, the more modern he became, and the more successful at developing a modern equivalent to the great achievements of the poets of the past.

This book comes along at a time when I think readers may be in some danger of losing touch with the particular achievements of Yeats's greatest volumes. Many students encounter him now in the form of a *Selected Poems*, which contains some of his finest poems but too seldom reflects the deliberate juxtapositions of lyrics that constituted such an important aspect of his poetic practice, at least from *Responsibilities* (1914) on. There is a newly issued (1983) version of Yeats's *Poems*—edited by Richard J. Finneran—which, though it has the laudable effect of correcting errors and clarifying some of the poet's ideas about arrangement, misleads readers about the Yeats canon by numbering all the poems, by crowding them together, and by including uncollected poems in the latter part of the book. On the whole the book tends to blur the idea of what the collected poems were to be.

Given those handicaps, I wish that all readers of this book might have the privilege of inspecting a first edition of *The Tower* (New York: Macmillan, 1928). Its dust jacket and cloth binding, designed by T. Sturge Moore in consultation with Yeats, shows an image of the Norman tower at Ballylee that Yeats had bought and was restoring (fig. 1). Moore's image of the tower is simple and severe, but it is doubled by its reflection in the water. The central panel is surrounded by a design of geometric bars and rectangles, and the whole effect is strongly suggestive of the style now called art deco. Since Yeats's own stylistic shift from early to late is reminiscent of the modification from art nouveau to art deco, the cultural signals of the original book, for those who cared to read them, were both strong and accurate.

Inside the attractive cover, the reader of the original edition of *The Tower* found a deceptively simple table of contents: twenty-one poems and some notes. The look and feel of

Fig. 1. T. Sturge Moore's 1928 cover design for *The Tower*.

The Tower are in no way as challenging as those of the first edition of Joyce's *Ulysses* or Eliot's *The Waste Land* or Pound's *A Draft of XXX Cantos*. But this book asks as much, or more, from its readers; even now, some fifty-eight years later, the reading of *The Tower* in its entirety, given the difficulty of individual poems and the challenge of taking their interactions and sequence seriously, remains a considerable enterprise.

Unless otherwise indicated, I will draw my quotations from that first edition of *The Tower*, following its spelling and punctuation and order. Quotations from other volumes are drawn from Finneran's *Poems of W. B. Yeats: A New Edition* (London and New York: Macmillan, 1983).

A number of people have aided my work on this project but I wish to acknowledge a particular indebtedness to two colleagues, John Hobbs and David Walker. Their close and patient reading of the manuscript, at various stages and more than once, has been enormously helpful. To them, and to students and colleagues who have shared my interest in these poems over the years, my warm and heartfelt thanks.

1. Affinities
and Juxtapositions

We may begin our study of *The Tower* by considering
Yeats's position and activities as an artist in the 1920s, the
decade after the First World War in which most of the poems
in *The Tower* were written. I said in the Preface that Yeats is
sometimes seen as beyond the cultural "entanglements" most
poets reflect. Actually, far from being free of cultural obliga-
tions and affinities, Yeats had a surplus of them. He was com-
mitted to Irish nationalism, in politics and in literature, and
that often-stormy relationship had led, by the time *The Tower*
was published in 1928, to his serving as a senator in the newly
independent Irish Republic. He could look with considerable
satisfaction on the prospect of his native country being free at
last from centuries of English rule.

At the same time, Yeats was an English poet who had moved
all his life in English literary circles. He identified his work
with a tradition that included Shakespeare, Milton, Swift,
Blake, and the English Romantics. He had grown up in con-
tact with Pre-Raphaelites like William Morris and was very

much at home with the Aesthetic Movement of the 1890s, as represented by men like Oscar Wilde. By 1928 he had been, for a considerable period of time, one of England's leading lyric poets, probably *the* leader.

Indeed, the major symbols of *The Tower* are quite familiar to anyone who knows the English literary tradition. One can find, for example, among the minor poems of Spenser ("The Ruines of Time," "The Teares of the Muses," etc.), the tower, the swan, the centaur, the holy city, the paradise of artifice, the poet as dreamer and visionary, the golden image, and the chorus of muses. It is a familiar poetic vocabulary, transported, of course, to a world where "the center cannot hold." But its familiarity exhibits a calculated relation to the tradition.

As if these commitments and connections were not enough, Yeats also considered himself a European intellectual, conversant with an international artistic culture that had moved steadily, in the years before and after the First World War, into a new commitment to experimentation and unprecedented creativity in the arts, a commitment that jeopardized the standard definition of the artist's relation to society by attempting a dramatic redefinition of its terms and possibilities. Writers like James Joyce and Ezra Pound had more obvious connections with the community of European modernists than did Yeats, but we have only to compare the careers of more strictly Irish poets like A.E., or more strictly native English lyricists like Hardy, Hopkins, and Housman, to see how extensive and long-standing Yeats's connection with symbolist and postsymbolist literary culture had been by the time he assembled the poems of *The Tower*.

The award to Yeats of the Nobel Prize for Literature in 1923 may have signaled recognition of his service to all three cultures. Certainly it uncovered some of the uneasy tensions that had marked that triple allegiance. Some English critics grumbled about his getting the prize instead of Thomas Hardy. They assumed that a fashionable European interest in Ireland explained the award, not fully recognizing the substantial contribution to international modernism Yeats had made since his emergence from the "Celtic twilight" of his early poetry. By the same token, many Irish nationalists saw Yeats's nationalism as shallow and fitful, not least because it had come to avoid parochial concerns like the revival of Gaelic and the idealization of folk culture. Meanwhile, James Joyce, who had chosen a life of exile in centers of European modernism like Paris and Geneva, must have felt he had "outflanked" Yeats on at least one front: he would always be more emphatically identified with that world and its values than his older countryman.

Yeats's varied cultural allegiances, then, brought differing aesthetic commitments into direct conflict. The aesthetic of nationalism presumably defined art as subservient to the political, historical, and imaginative needs of a culture struggling to preserve and foster its identity. The values of the English poetic tradition argued a broader affinity: to literary excellence, to historical significance, and to the long poem as the vehicle of greatness in a tradition stretching, by means of neoclassical values, all the way back to Homer. But the international movement in the arts that had begun with symbolism in the late nineteenth century and had evolved— through such offspring as dadaism, cubism, futurism, and imagism—into an emphatic modernism disallowed the claims of national cultures and neoclassical traditionalism, stressing instead the fundamental independence of the artist. Instead of being bound by cultural claims of one kind or another the artist was free (though this constituted a claim in its own right) to forge new definitions of cultural meaning, redefining values by creating new forms, new objects, and new modes of perception. Anything less than fierce independence and radical experimentation was apt to be seen as compromise.

To simplify Yeats's conflicts by way of clarifying them, we can say that his nationalism told him to write for and about Ireland, his ties with English literary culture told him to achieve greatness by writing formal lyrics and long poems of ambitious scope, and his identity as a symbolist-turned-modernist told him to create radically new forms and ways of perceiving the world in the service of art.

His response to these multiple claims was complex and lifelong, but it is summarized and exemplified in the achievement of *The Tower*, his finest single volume. Yeats found that he could deal more effectively with his conflicts by dramatizing them than by concealing or ignoring them. Again and again he presents himself in his poems as a man torn by opposing loyalties and impulses, beleaguered by a reality too harsh and complex for an artist to confront successfully. But by the paradox of creation and the triumph of imaginative form, the "Yeats" inside the poems, whose failures are stressed and whose conflicts are usually unresolved, gives way to the Yeats outside them, their maker and shaper, whose artistic success is born, phoenixlike and paradoxically, from the personal disappointments and conflicting claims of the human life on which the poems are founded.

Thus, the "Yeats" who inhabits the poems of *The Tower* lives in Ireland, writes about it, survives its Civil War, and is uncertain about his artistic allegiance to it. Sometimes he wishes he could sail off to a holy city of the imagination based on the historical Byzantium. Entrapment in old age becomes a recurrent metaphor for his uneasy and inevitable relationship with his native land.

In formal terms *The Tower* is a collection of lyric poems, and a reader might naturally assume from that that Yeats is unable or unwilling to sustain a long poem in the manner of a Milton, or even a Wordsworth or a Tennyson. Sooner or later, however, readers of *The Tower* begin to realize that the very careful arrangement of short, disparate, and apparently separate poems achieves a unity and a scope that are equivalent, although different from and perhaps superior to, the unity and scope of the traditional long poem. Images echo and modify one another. A question posed by one poem may be answered by the next. Themes and motifs appear and reappear in a steadily expanding revelation of purpose and control. Just as the apparently helpless "Yeats" inside the poems is superseded by the master artist who shapes and survives them, so the lyrist who disperses himself among many short poems is displaced by the cunning arranger who orders them and creates thereby the startling unity and bold drama of *The Tower*. The same principle, of course, applies to the whole of *The Collected Poems*, a literary document that is much closer to *The Prelude* or *The Divine Comedy* than anyone could have thought from a first glance.

The double achievement of founding successful art on the confusions and failures of life and of realizing unity from apparent fragmentation and disparateness places Yeats in the company of other great modernists who appear to be capable of simultaneously dismantling and reconstructing the world they live in. From the drama of his conflicting allegiances, in life and in art, Yeats drew a triumphant answer to the problem of being a poet in the fractured and bewildering world of the twentieth century. His solution still stands as the most profound and far-reaching of any modern poet.

In light of what has just been said, the order of the poems in any given Yeats collection, as well as in the whole of *The Collected Poems*, is an absolutely crucial matter. Yet no one would be apt to gather this from the existing body of commentary on the poet. The significant exception among the critics is Hugh Kenner. As long ago as 1958, he argued cogently that Yeats's poems were best understood by reference to their context in his collected work, where they explained and clarified each other. "The place to look for light on any poem," he wrote, "is in the adjacent poems, which Yeats placed adjacent to it because they belong there. And the unit in which to inspect and discuss his development is not the poem or sequence of poems but the volume, at least from *Responsibilities* (1914) to *A Full Moon in March* (1935)."[1]

Critics have, I think, recognized the importance of the individual volumes that make up Yeats's collected work, but they have not acted on the idea that the poet's careful ordering of poems deserves close attention, or that the best way to interpret individual poems is by context, through attention to the poems that surround them and a sense of their role in the unfolding drama of the volume to which they belong. Even Kenner contents himself mostly with pointing out the guiding principle of Yeats's art rather than using it to produce readings of particular poems.

To presume that the poems themselves, in their order within the volumes that make up *The Collected Poems*, are each other's best interpreters, is not only to assert their artistic interdependence and formal uniqueness; it is also to claim that the working principle behind the successful design of the Yeats canon is juxtaposition. The principle informs the mature work of Yeats at every level: word to word, image to image, stanza to stanza, section to section, poem to poem, and book to book, so that Yeats's *Collected Poems*, made up of discrete, coherent books of poetry standing in chronological relation to one another, is simply the largest example of an artistic method that operates on the smallest scale as well. The Yeatsian model of synapsis, relation, and exchange comes in every size, enacting a continuous drama. The "loose" organization of poems like "Meditations in Time of Civil War" is anything but casual when seen in this light. The reader is expected to participate boldly in the imaginative enterprise of such poems, inferring and exploring relations that are not made explicit.

A good example of the way this works may be found in the third section of "The Tower." The elderly poet is talking about making his will and declaring his faith. Between a glance at human accomplishment from the past and a continuation of his "testament," he inserts a stanza devoted to images of nesting birds:

I have prepared my peace
With learned Italian things
And the proud stones of Greece,
Poet's imaginings
And memories of love,
Memories of the words of women,
All those things whereof
Man makes a superhuman,
Mirror-resembling dream.

As at the loophole there,
The daws chatter and scream,
And drop twigs layer upon layer.
When they have mounted up,
The mother bird will rest
On their hollow top,
And so warm her wild nest.

I leave both faith and pride
To young upstanding men
Climbing the mountain side,
That under bursting dawn
They may drop a fly.

The reader's "problem" with the image of the daws is to decide how to fit it as a figure to the discourse that precedes and follows it. The "as" that introduces it is syntactically ambiguous. Is the nesting analogous to the human creativity Yeats has made his peace with? Or is it a metaphor for the testament making whereby he prepares the way for artists to come? Is the emphasis, in other words, on the building of the nest (a tower of a kind) or on the resting and warming that come after?

The "problem" is of course no problem at all when we understand Yeats's use of juxtaposition, here on the level of the stanza and the extended figure. The figure of the nesting daws confers meaning in both directions and constitutes a mysterious bridge between the art of the past, the poet facing death, and the art that has yet to be created. The activities of the birds have a timeless quality, but they exist in time, linking past to future. The structural and syntactical indeterminacy of the stanza is the very source of its richness. Its independence in the text defines, in effect, the nature of its interdependence.

A good reader of *The Tower* will also discover ways of relating the jackdaws not only to the passages immediately preceding and following them, but to other bird images that this one echoes and that will subsequently echo it in turn. And one can of course go beyond *The Tower*, to earlier and later volumes as well. The principle is illustrated by the image of the young men fishing. It echoes the opening of the poem, which by its diction echoed Wordsworth (thus bringing an earlier poetic "testament" to bear on the activities the poem surveys), but it also recalls a poem from *The Wild Swans at Coole*, "The Fisherman," in which the poet defiantly takes his destiny into his own hands by imaginatively creating his own audience. Art is indeed a "mirror-resembling dream" when associations and reflections multiply in this way, yet it is also an activity as natural to human beings as nesting is to birds, so that the effect of the open-ended analogy is both to tie the meditation to the immediate and the ordinary, and at the same time to increase its fundamental sense of wonder.

One implication of the Yeatsian reliance on the value of juxtaposition is a redefinition of the literary symbol. A symbol tends to stand grandly at the center of a text or passage and let meaning surround and enrich it. But Yeats is interested in something more dynamic. What is the tower at Ballylee, after which this book is titled, a symbol of? There is no reliable answer apart from each of its appearances in the unfolding drama of the collection and the implicit sum of their meanings. The rhythms of juxtaposition have replaced the central ordering effect of the symbol, and symbolic meanings shift as we move from poem to poem. Take, for example, the cradle that closes "The Second Coming" and that opens "A Prayer for My Daughter." Many readers have admired these poems independently, but few have noted that Yeats placed them in deliberate sequence in *Michael Robartes and the Dancer* (1921). "The Second Coming" is vivid and terrifying; in the course of pondering modern chaos its speaker is suddenly visited by an impersonal vision of gigantic cycles of historical change. That it should be followed by a poem that is personal, domestic, and a good deal more hopeful about the place of the individual among the cycles of time is not an accident but a careful juxtaposing, calculated to bring a larger truth from the conjunction of two poems than either could foster on its own. The linking image is the cradle, which must transform its own meaning in order to make the juxtaposition work. "The Second Coming" concludes:

> The darkness drops again; but now I know
> That twenty centuries of stony sleep
> Were vexed to nightmare by a rocking cradle,
> And what rough beast, its hour come round at last,
> Slouches toward Bethlehem to be born?

The image of the innocent cradle as the means whereby the monstrous sphinx is aroused is a part of the poem's horror; nothing is free from the convulsions of change, and the smallest things can serve to trigger them. A lesser poet would leave it at that, but Yeats is willing to turn right around and use the cradle again, as he opens "A Prayer for My Daughter":

> Once more the storm is howling, and half hid
> Under this cradle-hood and coverlid
> My child sleeps on. There is no obstacle
> But Gregory's wood and one bare hill
> Whereby the haystack- and roof-levelling wind,
> Bred on the Atlantic, can be stayed;
> And for an hour I have walked and prayed
> Because of the great gloom that is in my mind.

The kind of mood we might expect to be provoked by "The Second Coming" persists—in the second stanza Yeats admits to "imagining in excited reverie / That the future years had come, / Dancing to a frenzied drum, / Out of the murderous innocence of the sea." However, the fact that it is now set in familiar and domestic surroundings, that the cradle is that of the poet's own child, allows the poem to modulate to a degree of optimism by turning from political and historical versions of human experience to an emphasis on spiritual self-fulfillment:

> Considering that, all hatred driven hence,
> The soul recovers radical innocence
> And learns that it is self-delighting,
> Self-appeasing, self-affrighting,
> And that its own sweet will is Heaven's will;
> She can, though every face should scowl
> And every windy quarter howl
> Or every bellows burst, be happy still.

"The Second Coming" and "A Prayer for My Daughter" are beautifully whole and exciting poems, but it is when they are juxtaposed and their respective visions balanced—the drowned "ceremony of innocence" of the first revived in the

second as part of an unfolding drama of continuous specula-
tion and shifting emotion—that they realize their finest pos-
sibilities. To understand this fully the reader must accept
process over stability, participating in the exchanges of mean-
ing through which the Yeatsian world gains both its multi-
plicity and its ultimate coherence. And the critic, I am
suggesting, must pay the closest possible attention to the ges-
tures of arrangement and relationship by which the order of
the poems reveals the uniqueness, modernity, and particu-
larity of the poet's art.

To the casual reader of Yeats, it may look as though
The Tower appeared after an uncharacteristic silence. Yeats's
two previous volumes, *The Wild Swans at Coole* and *Michael
Robartes and the Dancer*, are dated 1919 and 1921 in *The Col-
lected Poems*, while *The Tower* is 1928, so that it is easy to
jump to the conclusion that the poet was productive at the
beginning of the decade and then experienced a slowdown
that created a seven-year gap between volumes. In fact,
the picture of Yeats's productivity during the 1920s is quite
different.

It had become Yeats's habit by this time in his life to move
toward the final arrangement of a volume of poems by dis-
tinct stages. Between their magazine publication and their
appearance in book form, in the volumes whose size and ar-
rangement are largely preserved in *The Collected Poems*,
Yeats's poems were generally published in shorter collections
that allowed him to experiment with their possibilities of
juxtaposition. Thus, the contents of *The Tower* had been
"tried out" in quite different arrangements in smaller collec-
tions, as follows:

Seven Poems and a Fragment-Cuala Press, 1922
   All Souls' Night
   On a Picture of a Black Centaur by Edmund Dulac

Nineteen Hundred and Nineteen
The New Faces
A Prayer for My Son
The Hero, the Girl, and the Fool
The Wheel
(A New End for 'The King's Threshold')

The Cat and the Moon and Certain Poems-Cuala Press, 1924
The Cat and the Moon (from *Wild Swans*, 1919)
Youth and Age
Leda and the Swan
Meditations in Time of Civil War
The Gift of Harun Al-Rashid
Owen Aherne and His Dancers

October Blast-Cuala Press, 1927
Sailing to Byzantium
The Tower
Wisdom
Two Songs from a Play
Among School Children
A Man Young and Old (under different titles)
The Three Monuments
From 'Oedipus at Colonus' (ultimately the last section of
    "A Man Young and Old") [2]

If the reader simply compares the order of the first four
poems in *The Tower*—"Sailing to Byzantium," "The Tower,"
"Meditations in Time of Civil War," and "Nineteen Hundred
and Nineteen"—with their separate appearances in the three
smaller volumes, or considers that "Among School Children"
was at one point between "Two Songs from a Play" and "A
Man Young and Old," whereas Yeats eventually put it be-
tween "On a Picture of a Black Centaur by Edmund Dulac"
and "Colonus' Praise" (the latter the only poem, incidentally,

making its first appearance in *The Tower*), it will begin to be clear how much consideration went into the final order of Yeats's poems in his major volumes, and how little he felt tied either to chronology or to precedent. We may note, too, something like the evolution of the volume, for as the pamphlets grow closer to it in time their own order of contents tends to reflect that of the larger volume in which they will be placed; *October Blast* is a miniature *Tower* in a sense that cannot be claimed for the two earlier pamphlets.

In discussing an individual volume of *The Collected Poems*, the commentator must choose among several possibilities, as Yeats continued to experiment with small changes in the order of the poems right up to the end of his life. In considering *The Tower* I have decided to follow the order of the first edition, with one exception: the moving of "From 'Oedipus at Colonus'" from its original position (third to last) to become the final section of "A Man Young and Old." The first edition's order is otherwise the one that the reader will find in *The Collected Poems*, with two exceptions: a different placing of "Wisdom," and the inclusion of "The Gift of Harun Al-Rashid" as the next-to-last poem, rather than in the separate section of "Narrative and Dramatic" poems one finds in *The Collected Poems*. Both of these variations will be discussed in more detail at the appropriate junctures.

2. Byzantium and Back

Yeats chose to open *The Tower* with one of his greatest lyrics, "Sailing to Byzantium." The poem reflects the varying cultural affinities Yeats struggled with, and it introduces a number of the themes and some of the characteristic rhythms of thought and experience that pervade the volume. It also faces the reader with a number of interpretive problems, as if to demonstrate that apprehending the unity and dramatic energy of *The Tower* will be, again and again, a challenging task.

The form of "Sailing to Byzantium" is ottava rima, four stanzas of it, and since that form has strong associations with Byron (*Don Juan*, "Beppo," "The Vision of Judgment"), it gives the poem a firm grounding in the tradition of English poetry. So, in effect, does its affinity with the dramatic monologue, recalling the achievements of poets like Tennyson, Browning, and Hardy. Ottava rima is for Byron a vehicle for comic and satirical narrative; crossed with a poem that echoes the Victorian dramatic monologue it takes on a more

serious tone and a psychological emphasis, resembling a so-
liloquy by a tragic hero:

I

That is no country for old men. The young
In one another's arms, birds in the trees
—Those dying generations—at their song,
The salmon-falls, the mackerel-crowded seas,
Fish flesh or fowl, commend all summer long
Whatever is begotten born and dies.
Caught in that sensual music all neglect
Monuments of unaging intellect.

Both the term "sailing" and the demonstrative "that" sug-
gest that the country being rejected is close at hand, though
the next stanza will present the speaker as having already ar-
rived in Byzantium. The poem does not specifically identify
Ireland as the country in question, but since Yeats was old
and Irish, and since readers are apt to consider him, in the
absence of evidence to the contrary, as in some sense the
speaker, a second cultural affinity, Irish nationalism, is in-
voked by way of the speaker's rejection of his native land. We
know that in earlier versions of the poem Yeats had in mind a
medieval speaker, an Irish monk who persuades some "sun-
browned mariners" to take him to what was then the center
of Christian civilization.[3] Yeats's decision to erase the histori-
cal setting and blur the speaker's identity readied the poem
for its eventual role among the poems of *The Tower*, strength-
ening its connection to Yeats's own life and emotions as he
would use them in the book, but the change made the reader's
job more difficult. The choice of "Byzantium" as the destina-
tion of an unidentified speaker, who may be the modern poet
himself, becomes more mysterious; the city grows less his-
torical and more symbolic. The sense in which it is a "solu-
tion" to the problem of old age is more firmly imaginary:

II

An aged man is but a paltry thing,
A tattered coat upon a stick, unless
Soul clap its hands and sing, and louder sing
For every tatter in its mortal dress,
Nor is there singing school but studying
Monuments of its own magnificence;
And therefore I have sailed the seas and come
To the holy city of Byzantium.

The first two stanzas have blended reasoning with travel, so that the "arrival" at the end of the second stanza completes a syllogism: 1. Old age is paltry unless it is devoted to schooling the soul. 2. The way to school the soul is to study monuments of its achievement; Byzantium is both such a monument in itself and the location of such activity. 3. Therefore, an old man should sail to Byzantium.

The aesthetic behind the poem, we can now see, is that of the symbolist movement, which had stressed over and over the restless entrapment of the human spirit in an imperfect material world, and the artist's priestly role in ministering to the needs of that spirit and aiding in its liberation. Yeats had grown up with this aesthetic, and its values remained significant to him as a confirmation of the importance of art and a definition of the sacred mission of the poet, who could hope to soothe and nourish his own entrapped soul, along with those of the elect readers or viewers who had the courage to follow his spiritual and transcendental quest.

In the circumstances, it is not surprising that the poem now turns from reasoning to prayer:

III

O sages standing in God's holy fire
As in the gold mosaic of a wall,
Come from the holy fire, perne in a gyre,

And be the singing masters of my soul.
Consume my heart away; sick with desire
And fastened to a dying animal
It knows not what it is; and gather me
Into the artifice of eternity.

Here at its half-way point, the poem has somehow turned on itself and become more problematic. We thought that the speaker had solved his problems by deciding to abandon the country of change and go to the holy city. (The country-to-city move makes this poem a curious kind of antipastoral, idealizing civilization as against nature.) Instead, he seems to be in a sort of limbo, a threshold state where he must pray to "sages" already in eternity for release from his entrapment in his own body. The analogue to this situation is of course the Christian's prayer to be taken into heaven, but that this paradise is associated more with aesthetic than religious rewards is indicated by the fact that the sages seem to be part of a splendid mosaic, of the kind Yeats saw in Ravenna and associated with Byzantine art at its finest, and the fact that eternity itself is somehow an "artifice." Does that make eternity identical with Byzantium, or does it mean that only something as artificial as a city, one filled with artistic accomplishments, can even be the portal to a more perfect and less changeful world? The reader is invited to ponder these questions.

Sooner or later, in fact, readers must consider that this poem is about the relation between artist and work of art. The latter can be perfect and changeless, while the former is subject to decay and mortality. Old age makes the problem especially acute, and that dilemma will pervade this volume by a sixty-three-year-old poet, desperate to reconcile his deteriorating physical condition with the energy and mastery of his imagination and the increasing power of his poems.

One "solution" is an escape from the world of change to a singing school of spiritual rapture on the threshold of eternity. The speaker of this poem sounds rather confident about his ultimate success:

> IV
> Once out of nature I shall never take
> My bodily form from any natural thing,
> But such a form as Grecian goldsmiths make
> Of hammered gold and gold enamelling
> To keep a drowsy emperor awake;
> Or set upon a golden bough to sing
> To lords and ladies of Byzantium
> Of what is past, or passing, or to come.

With his next incarnation picked out, both a fabulous object and a continuation of his status as a singer-poet, the speaker would appear to have his problems resolved.

But there are, as many readers and commentators have noticed, hidden and not-so-hidden problems. The speaker wants to escape from his body, "a dying animal," but his bodily form in the next world will be that of an animal, or an object emulating animal form and behavior—a singing bird. His urge to escape this world comes from the recognition that he is "sick with desire" (or rather, technically, his heart is) and wishes to be purged of it. But the whole poem is an expression of desire, a passionate longing to be rid of the burdens of old age and mortality, to merge with a world of artistic and eternal perfection. Will transcendental desires really operate when the heart finally "knows" what it is, or are they a function of the bitter human heart?

Most paradoxical of all, of course, is the fact that the speaker is still trapped in process. He has needed it to get from the turbulent world of sensual music and dying generations to his threshold status in Byzantium, and he must now beg the sages to "consume" his heart away and "gather" him into eternity. If that is accomplished, the eternal form he plans to adopt, that of a golden bird keeping "a drowsy emperor awake" (eternity sounds just a bit on the dull side), recalls the first stanza's birds. The triad they commend all summer long, "Whatever is begotten born and dies," turns into a song that recounts "what is past, or passing, or to come," specifically returning time to eternity and suggesting that process is impossible to escape, at least in the imagination and language of the speaker.

There was a time when this effect would have been called "ironic," the undercutting of the speaker's point of view by the language and imagery of the poem. Nowadays, such a reading would be called "deconstructionist," demonstrating that the poem, either through the inadequacies of verbal expression or the artist's incomplete control of his art and entrapment in his cultural biases, falls short of its stated aims and ideals. No doubt there will in time be other terms for this kind of second perception, this turning of a literary text back upon itself to create problems just when it seemed to have resolved them. Whatever name we give the effect, it was such a characteristic Yeatsian practice by the time of *The Tower* that its presence in "Sailing to Byzantium" constitutes a superb introduction to the world of Yeats's poetry, a world of ebb and flow, success and failure, confidence and despair. The rhythm can occur from one poem to the next, as it will in the movement from "Sailing to Byzantium" to "The Tower," but it is also important to recognize that it is really built into "Sailing" itself, a poem that is somehow both a triumphant declaration of artistic independence and an admission that neither art nor the artist can truly transcend time, only imagine and dream such transcendence: both a solution to the problem of old age and a recognition that the problem is insoluble. What is strange is that the poem's contrary impulses, its tendency to "deconstruct," do not mark it as a failure but rather increase our sense of exhilaration and comprehensiveness.

Whatever else one says about "Sailing to Byzantium," the poem did seem to leave its aged speaker in a distant holy city, poised to enter a paradise of the imagination. The counterrhythm to that comes in the poem that follows. Not only is the speaker of "The Tower" still plagued by old age, he is also back in Ireland, the country where an old man is on the wrong side of a cycle of begetting, birth, and death. The effect of the shift, even after we recognize the built-in qualifications of "Sailing," is both violent and dramatic:

> What shall I do with this absurdity—
> O heart, O troubled heart—this caricature,
> Decrepit age that has been tied to me
> As to a dog's tail?

There is clearly to be no easy progress in *The Tower*, and no evasions: the restatement of a problem, the reengagement with the frustration of aging without any anticipated escape from nature—these signal the presence of a dialectical method that will ebb and flow between poems as well as within them.

Moving from "Sailing" to "The Tower," then, we keep certain themes as constants—age as a personal difficulty, time as a metaphysical problem—even as we shift our ground. A different setting, a different voice and tone, a somewhat altered prosody. The speaker is now more clearly identified with the poet, considering his situation in the present. The manner is still that of soliloquy, but the style is both more hectic and more drawn out. The formal assurance of ottava rima has given way, in the first section, to fused quatrains whose formality is far less apparent. Stresses fall heavily, and the diction veers from formal to informal, homely to exalted, with elements of parody (of Wordsworth, especially, in "the humbler worm"): [4]

> Never had I more
> Excited, passionate, fantastical
> Imagination, nor an ear and eye
> That more expected the impossible—
> No, not in boyhood when with rod and fly,
> Or the humbler worm, I climbed Ben Bulben's back
> And had the livelong summer day to spend.
> It seems that I must bid the Muse go pack,
> Choose Plato and Plotinus for a friend
> Until imagination, ear and eye,
> Can be content with argument and deal
> In abstract things; or be derided by
> A sort of battered kettle at the heel.

As this serves to qualify "Sailing to Byzantium" and its hope for an easy transition from natural to supernatural, so can the former poem serve to give us a slight distance on the rage and frustration that open "The Tower." The distance is also present in the discourse of the opening section by means of half-humorous touches ("go pack," "a sort of battered kettle") and the implicit qualification of Wordsworth's pastoral idylls of childhood, but it is surely reinforced by the fact that the poem whose speaker can ask "What shall I do" has been preceded by one that seemed closer to having an answer. This counterbalancing, which is quite typical of the deliberate juxtaposing of *The Tower*, makes for a complexity of tone, a multiplication of possibilities and points of view, that is difficult—the reader must bear many things in mind at once—but enormously rewarding.

"The Tower" goes on to work out its own resolution, and if we ultimately feel that it corresponds to the resolution in the first poem, that will not be before we have encountered many differences. Imaginative mastery begins to reassert itself in the second section of the poem, as the old poet, pacing the battlements of his tower, summons the images he needs for his answer to the opening question ("What shall I do with this absurdity?"). His imagination moves from the present landscape—foundations of a house, "Tree, like a sooty finger"—into history—Mrs. French, the peasant girl "commended by a song" and the men who "maddened by those rhymes / Or else by toasting her a score of times" came to disaster when "one was drowned in the great bog of Cloone." He pauses to express a hope for his art—that it have the apparent potency of the rhymes by the blind man who celebrated the peasant girl—and then summons an image not from the actuality of present landscape or past history, but from his own creative imagination: "And I myself created Hanrahan." The fact that the speaker is a working artist with a history of successful creation has now been brought directly to bear on his opening dilemma. Nature, history, folklore, and the passionate imagination have been presented in a fashion that gives them equivalent reality and comparable value.

But the progression is not easy, and has not been completed. Yeats (by which I mean of course the voice he has constructed here to speak the poem) cannot remember all of Hanrahan's story—old age is also plagued by forgetfulness—and he returns to history: "I must recall a man . . . / An ancient bankrupt master of this house." That master's "dog's day" and bankruptcy connect him to the speaker, hounded by old age and a sense of artistic and spiritual impoverishment. And the imaginative mastery that has been expressed in the speaker's confidence about summoning presences from the past and the imagination is shown to exist in tension with the fact that images may come unbidden and unwelcome:

And certain men-at-arms there were
Whose images, in the Great Memory stored,
Come with loud cry and panting breast
To break upon a sleeper's rest
While their great wooden dice beat on the board.

Yeats presents himself as a kind of Prospero, capable of special powers but having an uneasy relation with them, a control that may be temporary or precarious. At any rate, he is now ready to question them:

As I would question all, come all who can;
Come old, necessitous, half-mounted man;
And bring beauty's blind rambling celebrant;
The red man the juggler sent
Through God-forsaken meadows; Mrs. French,
Gifted with so fine an ear;
The man drowned in a bog's mire,
When mocking muses chose the country wench.

All of these phantoms begin to seem like confused and ironic versions of the speaker, so that he is one and many:

Did all old men and women, rich and poor,
Who trod upon these rocks or passed this door,
Whether in public or in secret rage
As I do now against old age?
But I have found an answer in those eyes
That are impatient to be gone;
Go therefore; but leave Hanrahan,
For I need all his mighty memories.

The implied answer is yes and is manifested in the spirits' impatience. Only the phantom who is in fact Yeats's own imagining can be bidden to stay for questioning. And to question Hanrahan is a dramatized way for the poet to question himself. There are both comic and serious meanings at work:

how a figment of the poet's own imagination can know any-
thing more than he knows may puzzle us, but if we put it in
terms of art's superiority to the artist—it is more finished,
more unified and self-contained—what we have is a serious
paradox rather than a joke.

In the last two stanzas of section 2, Yeats presents Hanra-
han as an expert on love, an "Old lecher" who has "Reckoned
up every . . . Plunge . . . / Into the labyrinth of another's
being," and asks him:

> Does the imagination dwell the most
> Upon a woman won or woman lost?

Readers who know the body of poetry that precedes *The
Tower* will feel justified in finding in the question this mean-
ing among others: now that Yeats is happily married in real-
ity, is there any reason why he need be victimized by the un-
consummated passion for Maud Gonne? And the answer,
presented hypothetically, is that if the imagination is domi-
nant, as it must be in both poet and lecher, then the hypo-
thetical, the "woman lost," will continue to preoccupy both
the poet and his creation:

> If on the lost, admit you turned aside
> From a great labyrinth out of pride,
> Cowardice, some silly over-subtle thought
> Or anything called conscience once;
> And that if memory recur, the sun's
> Under eclipse and the day blotted out.

Earlier in the poem, Yeats had hoped that moon and sunlight,
imagination and reality, might seem "One inextricable beam"
as it had for the men who responded to Raftery's verses about
Mary Hines. But the emphasis here is on the helplessness of
the artist, victim of his own strong imagination and of other

human qualities like pride, cowardice, and conscience, blind like Raftery and at the mercy of obsessive memories. Yeats's honesty arouses admiration, but the poem seems to have made no progress toward resolving the difficulties presented in section 1. The fact that "Never had I more / Excited, passionate, fantastical / Imagination" seems to hinder rather than aid the aging artist, as it draws him to the past and makes his old age a fading retrospection of his youth.

In section 3, however, we are given the other side of the matter. It is as if Yeats's honesty about his unwilling victimization by imagination has suddenly allowed him resilience and release. The acceptance of imagination's limits now opens the way for a celebration of its rewards. Juxtaposition is again the means by which one mood and truth give way to another. Without any transition as smooth as the ones used in "Sailing to Byzantium," the speaker appears to change the subject and busy himself with something else: "It is time that I wrote my will." This trope has several functions: it seems to come out of a resignation to age and death, but leads to a triumphant review of the accomplishments that can be part of an artist's legacy. The word "will" itself contains the dual possibilities of resignation and self-assertion. And the idea of a testament, with its strong religious overtones, leads on to a declaration of belief that joins the poem's triumphant crescendo:

> Pride, like that of the morn,
> When the headlong light is loose,
> Or that of the fabulous horn,
> Or that of the sudden shower
> When all streams are dry,
> Or that of the hour
> When the swan must fix his eye
> Upon a fading gleam,
> Float out upon a long

Last reach of glittering stream
And there sing his last song.

This extended definition of pride, part of the legacy that he can pass on, encompasses both dawn and twilight, as well as the weather of excess, drought, and flood, associating them with Roland's last heroic gesture and its link to the swan's sudden eloquence at the approach of death. The catalogue is a crafty one, combining literary tradition, folklore, and images from the world of natural process, and it helps prepare us for the violent humanism that follows:

And I declare my faith;
I mock Plotinus' thought
And cry in Plato's teeth,
Death and life were not
Till man made up the whole,
Made lock, stock and barrel
Out of his bitter soul,
Aye, sun and moon and star, all,
And further add to that
That, being dead, we rise,
Dream and so create
Translunar Paradise.

This is an astonishing set of assertions for a poet whom many have taken to be a thoroughgoing mystic and spiritualist, with an elaborate—an overelaborate —belief in the supernatural, in extrahuman powers and presences. The dismissal of Plato and Plotinus will be qualified in a note, but they are mostly rhetorical opponents anyway, representatives of those who fail to see how central the human imagination is to the whole of creation. To say that "man made up the whole" and that we raise ourselves from the dead and "dream" into existence a paradise beyond change is to put the phrase "artifice of eternity" from the previous poem in a whole new light. It shifts the responsibility for harmonious and meaningful creation onto the human imagination. The "Great Memory" mentioned earlier is, it turns out, human memory, and we need not feel alien from its images. Yeats does not come to rest on this declaration of independence—the dialectical procedures of his poetry would not allow that—but the assertion that "man made up the whole" (supported by the wonderfully homely diction of "lock, stock and barrel") should not be forgotten by any reader of The Tower. It implies that human creation is at one with the rest of creation—life, death, sun, moon, star—is indeed the source of everything, and that makes possible the summary of art's nature and power, and the resolving trope, discussed earlier, where a poet's life and legacy, his relation to a continuous tradition, are no different from the activities of nesting birds. Art and nature close their gap, as do natural and supernatural.

The key phrase that ends the list and the long stanza deserves our attention:

All those things whereof
Man makes a superhuman
Mirror-resembling dream.

Can it be superhuman if man makes it? The paradox is central to The Tower; it is the demand Yeats makes of art. "Mirror-resembling dream" suggests a similar tension between solipsism and an objective reflecting of the world in "mirror-resembling," while "dream," a favorite Yeatsian term, is charged with the dual possibilities of "illusion" and "ideal." Language controlled so superbly is its own best testament of success, so that Yeats can seem to belittle the bustle of the artist ("The daws chatter and scream, / And drop twigs layer upon layer") without in fact shaking our confidence, which is founded securely on his ability to be comprehensive without apparent strain. The imagery of birds, along with other images of natural harmony, contributes to the sense of continuity in the poem's quiet close:

> Now shall I make my soul
> Compelling it to study
> In a learned school
> Till the wreck of body
> Slow decay of blood,
> Testy delirium
> Or dull decrepitude,
> Or what worse evil come—
> The death of friends, or death
> Of every brilliant eye
> That made a catch in the breath—
> Seem but the clouds of the sky
> When the horizon fades;
> Or a bird's sleepy cry
> Among the deepening shades.

The first thing that might strike us about this passage is that where the speaker in "Sailing to Byzantium" was out in search of "sages" who could be "singing masters" of his soul, the speaker of this poem feels a quiet confidence that he can undertake to make his soul on his own. The "singing school" becomes a learned school, and the whole process of reconciliation shifts from the drama of escape through a faraway holy city to a gradual merging with local nature.

The tone of this poem's close is ambiguous, and can be read as bitter resignation. My own sense of it, however, is based on the quietly triumphant way in which the poem's persona, Yeats the speaker, begins to merge with the artisan who has designed it all, Yeats the maker. This kind of reconciliation of the self inside the poem and the self outside wasn't really possible in "Sailing to Byzantium," for all that poem's declarations of vigor and confidence. This closure seems more valid, less forced.

I am no doubt influenced in this reading by the modification of the symbolist tradition the poem has accomplished. The "swan song" of a moment earlier has given way to a less dramatic and more ordinary evocation of natural life, just as symbols have given way to juxtaposed images. The nesting daws and sleepy birds belong not so much to literary tradition as to the landscape around Thoor Ballylee. They are part of a twilight that reflects the earlier ideal of merging moonlight and sunlight but is also simply a rural Irish sunset in which the troubles of life fade out along with the horizon. The naturalness and homeliness of the ending represent a modernizing of the lyric that was part of Yeats's own shift away from symbolist and Aesthetic Movement mannerisms toward a more direct and informal manner that is part of the legacy of the imagist movement and the sensibility we define as modern. Yeats is still interested in spiritual transcendence, but he is here able to use natural imagery to express a supernatural idea. The golden bird—artifact, symbol, and archetype—has become a real bird, a natural sound in a natural countryside.[5]

3. Empty Houses

The careful reader of "Sailing to Byzantium" and "The Tower" will have noticed that they are followed by dates: 1927 and 1926 respectively. Seeing the title of the next poem, "Meditations in Time of Civil War," and knowing something about Irish history can easily lead one to look ahead to the date 1923 at the end of that poem, and to the fourth poem in the collection, which is titled "Nineteen Hundred and Nineteen" and has that date at its conclusion. Thereafter the dating is intermittent in the collection, but the reverse chronology of the first four poems is unmistakable.[6] Although this may partly be intended to remind us that Yeats is not bound by chronology in ordering his work, it also indicates that the forward movement of the collection is simultaneously, at the outset, a movement backward in time, through civil war and historical disillusionment, as if history in the twenties had a powerful undertow that the poetic imagination could not escape. The comparative triumphs of the first two poems, personal and self-contained, must now give way to the forces of historical and political circumstance, and the question will be how the poet's imagination can fare, or survive, when such forces predominate. In a way, the issue is already resolved by the date of the volume and the dating of the first poems: Yeats has come through. But in another sense the whole drama must be reenacted, so that the reader will experience it fully, and so that the resolutions Yeats has arrived at may be tested once again.

That comparatively tranquil activities like meditation should still be possible in a time of civil war is encouraging in itself, and indeed the events of 1922 and 1923 were probably less disturbing than those of a few years earlier, in the time of the Black and Tans. Still, the suggestions of self-division and self-destruction, when mixed with the interiorizing emphasis of "meditations," point to a time of crisis for both the self and the state. Yeats will scarcely depict violence until late in the sequence, and the "phantoms of hatred" he sees will have a reality as great as that of "the dead young soldier in his blood," but he will attend throughout to a sense of crisis—in personal continuity, in civilized values, in the ideas of regression and personal helplessness before historical forces—that seems bitter and profound.

In terms of the multiple cultural allegiances Yeats liked to balance, this poem suggests another sort of crisis, concerned mostly with the problems of Ireland and Irish nationalism. Yeats can glance at his other affinities and commitments, but he is both literally entrapped—he and his family were anxiously pinned down at Thoor Ballylee in the summer of 1922, while fighting raged around them—and spiritually encumbered by Irish politics and internecine enmity. The country he had tried to help liberate and shape a culture for threatens not only to be engulfed by fratricide, but to fetter the poet's imagination in the process. If "The Tower" brought poet and reader home from Byzantium, it still left the poet relatively free to celebrate imagination and formulate his artistic legacy. That freedom is threatened now, and we sense the threat even in the looser and more problematic form of the poem.

"Meditations" is one poem and it is seven poems. As a sequence with its own dialectic of images and ideas, it is of course a model of the larger work it belongs to, a kind of collection within the collection, like the later sequence "A Man Young and Old." Both sequences confront us with the question of what constitutes unity, and more specifically with whether a group of linked lyrics can "add up" to a successful whole. In this case, civil war seems to be threatening poetic form, but if we understand the miraculous unity of *The Tower* and earlier volumes, and of the important precedent of exploratory sequences like "Upon A Dying Lady," we are apt to have confidence in the resolution of this structural crisis, seeing in it instead a clue to the larger order of the volume we are reading.

The opening poem of this sequence, *"Ancestral Houses,"* challenges the imaginative self-sufficiency Yeats had developed in the final section of "The Tower." Thoor Ballylee itself, a fortress, a nest, a point of survey, is now questioned: can it retain a function and meaning in the midst of social uprooting and the evidence of civilization's decay? Self-sufficiency may be a crucial ideal to the poet ("Yet Homer had not sung / Had he not found it certain beyond dreams / That out of life's own self-delight had sprung / The abounding glittering jet"), but history suggests that it cannot be handed on, as Yeats's "will" had hoped to presume. The fountain can stand for realized achievement, but its persistence through time is questionable. England and Ireland both had manifold examples available of the dry and empty fountains around once-great houses. Yeats, letting us watch him choose among possibilities, deliberately substitutes a new symbol:

> . . . though now it seems
> As if some marvellous empty sea-shell flung
> Out of the obscure dark of the rich streams,
> And not a fountain, were the symbol which
> Shadows the inherited glory of the rich.

The seashell is of course an empty house, subject to the waters rather than controlling them, the opposite of the apparently self-sustaining and self-renewing fountain. And "*Ancestral Houses,*" using elaborate, encompassing syntax, faces the fact that the greatness needed to found dynasties or create great architecture and art can be vitiated by its own strengths, its violence and bitterness turning to self-destruction and war.

We recall that it was man's "bitter" soul that was the source of all creation in "The Tower." The creation, meant to assuage the bitterness, has the additional effect, when it succeeds, of vitiating the creative power. This ironic perception that creativity is its own undoing is supported by the poem's rhetoric. Assertions are pressed until they sound sarcastic— "Surely among a rich man's flowering lawns . . . Life overflows without ambitious pains"—and questions contain their own answers ("What if . . . gardens . . . lawns and gravelled ways . . . / But take our greatness with our violence?"). Irony is compounded by the effect of the sequence's title: in a time of civil war "levelled lawns and gravelled ways / Where slippered Contemplation finds his ease" will indeed seem "Mere dreams, mere dreams!" Any "progression" in *The Tower* thus far seems to be toward retrenchment, with the poetic imagination involved in what we might call orderly retreat.

The next stopping place in the retreat is not some rich

man's ancestral estate, but "*My House*," where the landscape
is more appropriate to the mood of retrenchment:

> An acre of stony ground,
> Where the symbolic rose can break in flower,
> Old ragged elms, old thorns innumerable,
> The sound of the rain or sound
> Of every wind that blows.

The tower has become a kind of bastion of the imagination,
and the poet, though not a descendant of the man-at-arms
who founded the place (previously summoned in "The
Tower"), nevertheless hopes that it now represents something
that can be passed on in time to his "bodily heirs" if only in
the form of "Befitting emblems of adversity." Retrenchment,
dramatically reducing human hopes for a significant legacy,
appears to have won a respite from the forces of change and
loss. The situation seems to allow room both for a review of
the dwelling that doubled as a symbol in the previous poem,
and for an expansion of values to include a cultural heritage
as "*Il Penseroso's* Platonist" is invoked.

The third poem, "*My Table*," finds the poet sitting in his
tower with a gift (not a legacy) that seems to help him avoid
aimlessness because of its own successful passage through
time: "A changeless sword . . . In Sato's house, / Curved like
new moon, moon luminous, / It lay five hundred years."
Again, though, the poet's own honesty forces him to give
ground:

> Yet if no change appears
> No moon; only an aching heart
> Conceives a changeless work of art.

The dialectic of creation and destruction is incessant and
endless. We know about aching hearts and changeless works
of art from "Sailing to Byzantium" and from "The Tower." Yet

the Japan of Sato's sword has seemed a culture in which art could function as ancestral heritage, as Yeats had hoped, and "A marvelous accomplishment" was passed on "And through the centuries ran / And seemed unchanging like the sword." Another Byzantium, as it were, or at least an alternative to chaotic Ireland. But Yeats's doubts, as "seemed" suggests, persist, and the poem closes with an ambiguous portrait of an inheritor in that culture:

> For the most rich inheritor,
> Knowing that none could pass Heaven's door
> That loved inferior art,
> Had such an aching heart
> That he, although a country's talk
> For silken clothes and stately walk,
> Had waking wits; it seemed
> Juno's peacock screamed.

A sense of strain informs this picture; elegant appearance conceals the old war between changelessness and change. "Waking wits" require an "aching heart," and the scream of the peacock (a transformation of the peacock who "strays / With delicate feet upon old terraces" where a statue of Juno stands in "*Ancestral Houses*"), which was supposed to announce the millennium, time completing itself, is thrilling but ominous, with its own hints of destruction, as this passage from *A Vision* serves to indicate:

A civilisation is a struggle to keep self-control, and in this it is like some great tragic person, some Niobe who must display an almost superhuman will or the cry will not touch our sympathy. The loss of control over thought comes toward the end; first a sinking in upon the moral being, then the last surrender, the irrational cry, revelation—the scream of Juno's peacock.[7]

By moving away from the Ireland of ancestral houses and civil war to a meditation on a different civilization, "*My Table*" has expanded the scope of "Meditations in Time of Civil War" without losing sight of its central concern: if individual excellence can be achieved, has it any chance of preservation, can it become an inheritance? The careful balance of personal and impersonal concerns that characterized the opening poems of *The Tower* continues here.

"*My Descendants*" carries the debate forward by admitting that while the poet, "Having inherited a vigorous mind," has some hope of leaving "a woman and a man behind / As vigorous of mind," he cannot ignore natural process:

> Life scarce can cast a fragrance on the wind,
> Scarce spread a glory to the morning beams,
> But the torn petals strew the garden plot;
> And there's but common greenness after that.

If heritage must dissipate, the "symbolic rose" be scattered, that dissipation is easier to accept when it is closely linked to natural processes that we all experience and whose inevitability we take for granted. The second stanza recapitulates this consideration ("And what if my descendants lose the flower . . . ?"). This time the image from nature serves to recall the image of nesting birds used in "The Tower" when the poet began to consider the relation between artistic achievement and inheritance:

> May this laborious stair and this stark tower
> Become a roofless ruin that the owl
> May build in the cracked masonry and cry
> Her desolation to the desolate sky.

The tone has shifted here to a bitter resignation. Since the tower was roofless when Yeats bought it, it is not like an ancestral house, and living in such an "emblem of adversity" makes it easier for him to recognize that he and it may belong to cycles of historical change that take no regard of such smaller continuities as inheritance or social stability. The retrenchment completes itself in the third stanza, as the poet moves from the recognition of those larger cycles—"The Primum Mobile that fashioned us / Has made the very owls in circles move"—to a sense that the tower's meaning can finally be only immediate and personal:

> And I, that count myself most prosperous,
> Seeing that love and friendship are enough,
> For an old neighbour's friendship chose the house
> And decked and altered it for a girl's love,
> And know whatever flourish and decline
> These stones remain their monument and mine.

In the last three poems of the cycle the issue of inheritance will disappear, as the speaker is left to a consideration of his own situation and of the need for his imagination to come to terms with it. In a sense, we have come back round from the testament making that closed "The Tower" to the sense of personal dilemma that opened it, moving like the owls, "in circles."

In "*The Road at My Door*" the war intrudes directly. The aging poet encounters representatives of both sides, "An affable Irregular" and "A brown Lieutenant and his men," and while he is able to talk with both, listening to the macabre jokes of the one, and chatting about bad weather with the other, he is closed within himself and in his tower chamber, alone with his thoughts:

I count those feathered balls of soot
The moor-hen guides upon the stream,
To silence the envy in my thought;
And turn towards my chamber, caught
In the cold snows of a dream.

Birds continue to make their presence felt in the sequence, echoing images from the opening poems. The peacocks of sections 1 and 3 seem to have their counterparts in the moor-hens of 2 and 5, and the owl of 4. In section 2 ("*My House*") the moorhens were "stilted" and "scared by the splashing of a dozen cows." Here, though "balls of soot" at first glance, they suggest generation, the continuity of life in nature, an echoing of the inheritance theme in terms of the larger impersonal forces that move the owls in circles and send them to nest in ruins. We are now well-prepared for the imagery, if not perhaps the music, of the poem that follows.

"*The Stare's Nest by My Window*" combines grimness and ecstasy in a way that would not be possible without the cumulative effects of the sequence as a whole. Yeats now uses an image of an abandoned bird's nest in which honeybees are building, and "the empty house of the stare" is surely his own head too, the last refuge when ancestral houses and temporarily restored ruins have been abandoned. It houses the staring gaze of the observant and visionary poet, but that last place of retreat also seems in danger of becoming "some marvellous empty sea-shell" instead of a source of creativity, a fountainhead. The invitation to the bees, the refrain of every stanza, has an air of desperation. "The sweetness that all longed for night and day" in "*Ancestral Houses*" now takes this impersonal and natural form. Bees are an ancient symbol of creativity and spirituality, of swarming souls, as their honey is an ancient symbol of wisdom, but each of the poet's

summons to them issues from an increasing concern about
the circumstances of civil war:

> My wall is loosening . . .

> We are closed in, and the key is turned
> On our uncertainty . . .

> Last night they trundled down the road
> That dead young soldier in his blood . . .

> We had fed the heart on fantasies,
> The heart's grown brutal from the fare,
> More substance in our enmities
> Than in our love; oh, honey-bees
> Come build in the empty house of the stare.

As the poem faces meaningless violence and a social chaos
that may signal the end of civilization, it seems, in its com-
pressed, songlike movement, in the insistent music of its
rhymes, and in the expressive imagery of its refrain, to reach
for a corresponding creative strength, what Wallace Stevens
called a pressure from the imagination to match the in-
creased pressure of reality.[8] Out of the strong comes some-
thing sweet, and Samson's riddle of the lion and the hon-
eycomb suggests the way by which Yeats reminds himself that
"loosening masonry" and the decay of civilization may pro-
duce a corresponding greatness in the imagination. If crea-
tion is the force that brings on destruction, the opposite
effect is just as inevitable. Houses, nests, seashells, towers,
and heads may empty; they may also fill. A "terrible beauty"
is born, and we are both witnesses and participants.

Section 6 has constituted an emotional climax for "Medi-
tations." Lyric violence has answered civil violence. Refrain
has been used to summon a sense of order when chaos has

most threatened to take over. Impersonal natural forces have been invoked to remind us that creation and destruction finally interlock. And the use of "we" in the second and fourth stanzas has signaled the vital link between the poet and his tormented society. "We are closed in, and the key is turned / On our uncertainty" refers quite literally to the anxious Yeats family, listening to the neighborhood gunfire or watching the Republicans blow up the bridge near the tower, but it also speaks to the human condition in the same way that Eliot had in Section 5, lines 411 to 414, of *The Waste Land*:

> . . . I have heard the key
> Turn in the door once, and turn once only
> We think of the key, each in his prison
> Thinking of the key, each confirms a prison.

Essential human solitude is a conclusive insight for Eliot, a point of glum rest. For Yeats it is counterbalanced by his cultural and social commitments, which will not go away. The "we" of the fourth stanza must be understood to refer to the faction-ridden Irish people and to the decadent artists of Yeats's generation. Both have "fed the heart on fantasies" and seen it grow brutal; both must admit to "more substance in our enmities / Than in our loves." The admission of communal dilemma and communal responsibility balances the existential solitude, and that is important to recognize because the final, more visionary section of the poem will show us the poet alone with his phantoms. There are rhythms of solitude and community to be studied and understood, along with the rhythms of loosening masonry and building honeybees, and the last two lyrics of this sequence act them out.

The final section of "Meditations" is called "*I See Phantoms of Hatred and of the Heart's Fullness and of the Coming Emp-*

tiness," and is cast in the majestic, long-line visionary style Yeats used for some of his finest poems. It represents, as Whitaker suggests, "an ironic acceptance of the poet's vocation,"[9] for Yeats is here mostly the medium through which extraordinary images and truths can pass. The whole movement of "Meditations" has been from the personal to the impersonal: in terms of inheritance, of process and change, of tradition, and of art. Individual and cultural accomplishments are destroyed, and their energies scattered, while the impersonal energy of nature continues. We now find the poet, burdened with that knowledge, where we found him in the second section of "The Tower," summoning images and phantoms from his battlement:

> I climb to the tower top and lean upon broken stone,
> A mist that is like blown snow is sweeping over all,
> Valley, river, and elms, under the light of a moon
> That seems unlike itself, that seems unchangeable,
> A glittering sword out of the east.

Earlier images from the sequence—the luminous moon, the broken masonry, the ancient tower, the cold snows of a dream, the sword, the old ragged elms, the stream where cows and moorhens cross—are here reunited in a context where the poet seems capable of envisioning the interrelationship of changelessness and change. He knows what "seems" and what is "like" and "unlike," but he also sees beyond appearances. It is a disquieting state to be in:

> . . . A puff of wind
> And those white glimmering fragments of the mist sweep by.
> Frenzies bewilder, reveries perturb the mind;
> Monstrous familiar images swim to the mind's eye.

The head that houses the poet's "stare" is filling up. Personal feelings, questions of inheritance and habitation, even matters of survival and distinctions between life and death—these concerns disappear as the visionary state is temporarily granted to the poet. The monstrous images are also "familiar," in the magical sense of that word as well as in the way unwelcome presences can be somewhat comically "over-familiar," pressing their attentions on one. The impersonality of the process is emphasized by the absence of personal pronouns; it is "the mind" and "the mind's eye" that are involved now. In terms of his cultural entanglements, Yeats has entered a kind of "cultural float." He is claiming here to be connected to a kind of "overculture" that he elsewhere names the Great Memory.

Three visions follow, in the poem's middle stanzas. The first, an enraged mob calling for vengeance for the death of a man we have never heard of, offers a sharp perspective on the frantic immediacy and illusory reality of political passions. Once, nothing mattered more than the vengeance of this mob. Now it is a "senseless tumult," combining the present of Irish civil war, the historical past of France, and the frantic repetitions Dante encountered in hell:

> . . . In cloud-pale rags, or in lace,
> The rage driven, rage tormented, and rage hungry troop,
> Trooper belabouring trooper, biting at arm or at face,
> Plunges towards nothing, arms and fingers spreading wide
> For the embrace of nothing . . .

So powerful is the vision that the poet, "wits astray," is almost drawn into joining it.

The vision that succeeds it, of ladies riding on unicorns, seems diametrically opposed in its peace and beauty. But the ladies "close their musing eyes," and there is something narcotic, redolent of the decadents and aesthetes of the nineties, in their dreamy and elegant progress:

> . . . their minds are but a pool
> Where even longing drowns under its own excess;
> Nothing but stillness can remain when hearts are full
> Of their own sweetness, bodies of their loveliness.

The ladies have escaped the involvement in change that drives the mob "toward nothing," and have captured "The Sweetness that all longed for night and day" that the poem has been talking about since its opening section, but their absence of change is a nothingness in itself, seductive but frightening as it becomes "nothing but stillness." We miss the admixture of bitterness that drove artist, architect, and aristocrat to their ambiguous destinies.

The third vision, which we might expect to synthesize the extremes of the other two, is also the most mysterious. The poet sees "an indifferent multitude" which is syntactically the same as, or in adjunct to, "brazen hawks." I think the multitude are the same as the hawks, that we are meant to envision a whole sky of fierce birds who are indifferent to the preoccupations of the first two visions, "hate" and "pity" and "self-delighting reverie," leaving "Nothing but grip of claw, and the eye's complacency, / The innumerable clanging wings that have put out the moon."[10] Water hens, peacocks, owls, and stares here give way to daylight predators who can cast a cold eye (eye imagery is another uniting motif in this sequence) on the world they soar above and the prey they grasp in their talons. They may seem to combine changelessness with change, to express in natural terms the coldness (compare "the cold snows of a dream" in 5) and detachment the working poet must experience, but they are too destructive, finally, and too complacent to be equated with a visionary poet.

The speaker's indifference is also unhawklike because it is temporary. A man is not a hawk, and a poet, when he is not in the realm of the visionary, must return to his aching heart and go back down the stairs, descending to his labyrinth, as Yeats does in the closing stanza:

> I turn away and shut the door, and on the stair
> Wonder how many times I could have proved my worth
> In something that all others understand or share.

The poet's solitude makes him wistful (as at the end of "The Road at My Door"), but he recognizes that understanding and sharing would only have made his heart ache the more at the difference between ordinary knowledge and experience and the kind of visitation he has just had. Self-sufficient, free of illusions, he accepts his condition and its peculiarities:

> . . . The abstract joy,
> The half read wisdom of daemonic images,
> Suffice the ageing man as once the growing boy.

An affirmation of the self-sufficiency of the poetic imagination has been achieved once more, and again the immediate frustrations of age have been dissolved by a recognition that youth-age differences are superficial, even illusory.

"Meditations" is a difficult poem, by virtue of its length and scope, but an immensely rewarding one. It is leisurely and pessimistic, inclusive and candid. Our hopes for the survival through time of the things we cherish may be dismissed, and destruction shown to be the inevitable counterpart of creation, but there is something exhilarating about having such perceptions set forth so dramatically and effectively: we seem, like the poet on his tower-top in the fantastic moonlight, to be able to see fullness and emptiness, changelessness and change, with a kind of momentary "abstract joy" that is only possible through the cumulative effects of a carefully managed sequence, and that is intensified if we have come to "Meditations" after careful readings of "Sailing to Byzantium" and "The Tower."

4. A Requiem for Progress

"Nineteen Hundred and Nineteen," the fourth poem in *The Tower*, slides us backward four more years and into the bitterest insights of the whole collection. Ireland recedes somewhat as a subject. The bitterness stems of course partly from that part of Irish history known as the Troubles, but the larger context is that of the First World War and the destruction of an entire heritage, the breaking up of civilization. The kind of change Yeats is dealing with may well involve the dissipation of inherited wealth and the violence of civil war, but the scale is larger and the emphasis falls on the way in which great civilizations, since the time of the Greeks, have lost the objects and values that were most precious to them. The poem becomes a requiem for progress, both in the political sense—involving the faith in progress that had characterized English and European culture through the course of the nineteenth century—and in the realm of art—acknowledging the destruction of the symbolist heritage that Yeats himself had placed such faith in around the turn of the century.

The crisis of a civilization is thus mirrored in the crisis of its artists, artisans, and intellectuals, and the twofold dilemma makes personal, for the poet struggling to write the poem, what might otherwise be quite impersonal in its scale and scope.

The larger context is suggested at the outset by the examples of lost "things" the opening stanza contemplates:

> . . . There stood
> Amid the ornamental bronze and stone
> An ancient image made of olive wood—
> And gone are Phidias' famous ivories
> And all the golden grasshoppers and bees.

Yeats chooses the delicate and decorative artifacts of ancient civilizations rather than the more impressive monuments. Wood, ivory, and gold are the materials, rather than more substantial or durable "bronze and stone" nearby (though they too are "ornamental" rather than monumental). The reference recalls the "Grecian goldsmiths" of "Sailing to Byzantium," working in "hammered gold and gold enamelling" to make a miraculous replica of a bird in "an artifice of eternity"; it is also intended, I think, to evoke parallels with the civilization Yeats knew as a young man, the culture of the nineties and the fin de siècle, with its elaboration of design (what is now stylistically known as art nouveau), its art for art's sake doctrines, its love of elegance and high-spirited mimicry. As a survivor of it Yeats can look back on its foolishness and innocence with both irony and regret, and throughout "Nineteen Hundred and Nineteen" he draws on images—Loie Fuller, the swan, garlanded horses, bronzed peacock feathers—that evoke that world and its manners, the "great gazebo" he had himself helped to construct.[11] It is as though the fragility and intricacy of the artifacts of civilizations in their later stages themselves signal vulnerability to violence and decay, a process that was considered on a smaller scale in "Ancestral Houses," so that belief in progress becomes dangerously identified with these refined but fragile objects:

> We too had many pretty toys when young;
> A law indifferent to blame or praise,
> To bribe or threat; habits that made old wrong
> Melt down, as it were wax in the sun's rays;
> Public opinion ripening for so long
> We thought it would outlive all future days.
> O what fine thoughts we had because we thought
> That the worst rogues and rascals had died out.

Even an army is a kind of toy or harmless artifact in this sheltered world so confident of youth and progress:

> All teeth were drawn, all ancient tricks unlearned,
> And a great army but a showy thing;
> What matter that no cannon had been turned
> Into a ploughshare; parliament and king
> Thought that unless a little powder burned
> The trumpeters might burst with trumpeting
> And yet it all lack glory; and perchance
> The guardsmen's drowsy chargers would not prance.

The "drowsy chargers" will be transformed, like so much else that was part of that secure, confident world, into "phantoms of hatred . . . and the coming emptiness," but there will be no "terrible beauty" in the transformation, and the detachment of contemplating them as the "half-read wisdom of daemonic images" will in this case be difficult to maintain.

The next stanza draws the contrast between that past and

the poem's present more emphatically than at any time in "Meditations":

> Now days are dragon-ridden, the nightmare
> Rides upon sleep: a drunken soldiery
> Can leave the mother, murdered at her door,
> To crawl in her own blood, and go scot-free;
> The night can sweat with terror as before
> We pieced our thoughts into philosophy,
> And planned to bring the world under a rule,
> Who are but weasels fighting in a hole.

The most immediate reference here is to the Black and Tans in Ireland, but the images evoke atrocities from the Great War as well. The contrast between the aspirations of a civilization envisioning "the world under a rule" and the meaningless viciousness of "weasels fighting in a hole" gives the stanza scope at the same time that it makes it vividly unpleasant and reductive. One of the means by which the speaker in this poem seems more entrapped in the circumstances of historical disillusion and senseless violence is through Yeats's deliberate use, recalling the sixth section of "Meditations," of "we." He can not or will not separate himself from the credulous multitude who have had their pretty toys turned into nightmares.

The fifth stanza of section 1 moves from this "we," not to an "I" but to a hypothetical "he," a figure like the Yeats of the final section of "Meditations":

> He who can read the signs nor sink unmanned
> Into the half-deceit of some intoxicant
> From shallow wits; who knows no work can stand,
> Whether health, wealth or peace of mind were spent
> On master-work of intellect or hand,

No honour leave its mighty monument,
Has but one comfort left: all triumph would
But break upon his ghostly solitude.

This recapitulates the progression of "Meditations," the knowledge earned by retrenchment, the acceptance of the "ghostly solitude" that is the artist-visionary's lot, but the fact that it is "he" rather than "I" signals its inability to resolve the dilemma of this poem on a personal level. As the next stanza shows, the speaker is not ready to dissociate himself from other people; he is neither ghostly nor solitary:

But is there any comfort to be found?
Man is in love and loves what vanishes,
What more is there to say?

The section closes with the implication that all people know what "He who can read the signs" knows, and all are unwilling to face their knowledge:

          . . . That country round
None dared admit, if such a thought were his,
Incendiary or bigot could be found
To burn that stump on the Acropolis,
Or break in bits the famous ivories
Or traffic in the grasshoppers or bees?

All of the tensions and agonies that are the concern of "Nineteen Hundred and Nineteen" are expressed in this opening section and summarized in the line "Man is in love and loves what vanishes." The rest of the poem can be seen as variations—musical, formal, and imagistic—on this section, and as a kind of answer to the question, "What more is there to say?"

The second section puts us squarely in that world of fin de siècle and symbolist aestheticism, taking five lines to create a scene of eerie beauty, charged with the meanings of the poem's historical perspective, and five more to draw a metaphysical conclusion from the image:

When Loie Fuller's Chinese dancers enwound
A shining web, a floating ribbon of cloth,
It seemed that a dragon of air
Had fallen among dancers, had whirled them round
Or hurried them off on its own furious path;
So the platonic Year
Whirls out new right and wrong,
Whirls in the old instead;
All men are dancers and their tread
Goes to the barbarous clangour of a gong.

By now the juxtaposition of delicacy and brutality, of small scale and large perspective, has begun to seem natural to us, and the fate of the ivories and golden insects hovers around the lovely dancers as their ribbon turns to a dragon and begins to exercise its power over them. When the word "dancers" comes back for the third time, the shift in meaning seems unforced and inevitable. If personal elements recede into the background of this section—we feel that the speaker is telling an anecdote as he begins and then pulling back in order to glimpse the abstract patterns—what impresses us primarily is the rhetoric of "All men," connecting with the "Man is in love" of the previous section. The section itself is like a small and precious artifact, a bit of handiwork that paradoxically carries the vigorous message of its own perishability.

Section 3 employs the first person and a more meditative manner. The speaker seems deliberately vague, hunting and then choosing a traditional symbol that will allow him to move from "All men" to the question of the individual consciousness:

> Some moralist or mythological poet
> Compares the solitary soul to a swan;
> I am satisfied with that,
> Satisfied if a troubled mirror show it
> Before that brief gleam of its life be gone,
> An image of its state.

Whitaker calls this "troubled mirror" history; I think it points more toward art, the "mirror-resembling dream" that appeared to give the artist dominance through imagination in the second section of "The Tower," while it is here only a minor "comfort," a reflection that gives the solitary soul a knowledge of its own brevity in this tragic world.[12] But there is a magnificence in the "image of its state" that the mirror presents it with, a suggestion of immortality that counterbalances life's brevity:

> The wings half spread for flight,
> The breast thrust out in pride
> Whether to play, or to ride
> Those winds that clamour of approaching night.

This mirror is not the simple reflector of mimetic art that Yeats repeatedly repudiated; as "troubled" surface it is charged with historical meaning and a sense of "approaching night" that signals the death of the individual and society; as the water on which the swan floats, it is its very element, as the imagination is the artist's. In the stark surroundings of the poem, one cannot help but take courage from the image, reconstituted from the world of symbolist poetry and the

yellow nineties, the reconstituting itself a proof of the imagi-
nation's power to challenge and defy change. That the swan
may have the choice of "play" or riding the clamoring winds
may be one sort of tragic solace; "play" presumably includes
the manufacture of artifacts such as "Nineteen Hundred and
Nineteen" itself.[13]

The middle stanza goes further, however, and the endeav-
ors of imagination change from clarifying reflection to en-
cumbering labyrinth; "ghostly solitude" may itself be a con-
dition of entrapment:

> A man in his own secret meditation
> Is lost amid the labyrinth that he has made
> In art or politics.

Or love, we might add, remembering the image of sex as a
plunge "Into the labyrinth of another's being" in section 2 of
"The Tower." Lovers may lose themselves in the maze of the
other person, while artists and politicians construct their
own. Even a hermit who withdraws from the world will still
find himself in the maze of his own being, the "mummy-
cloth" wound around his own life and consciousness. Given
this inevitable entanglement, this losing of one's way, "Some
Platonist" (Yeats likes his persona to be vague about sources)
has argued that we must accept change totally, and repudiate
all our connections with this world, the self included. It is
better that our works should be destroyed since they tie us to
this world. Longing after beautiful artifacts and images is
simply the "ancient habit" we must unlearn:

> . . . if our works could
> But vanish with our breath
> That were a lucky death,
> For triumph can but mar our solitude.

But the speaker, as we know from "The Tower," is not ready to follow the Platonist's advice. In the third stanza the poem grows more personal as it turns round again to preoccupation with an image:

> The swan has leaped into the desolate heaven:
> That image can bring wildness, bring a rage
> To end all things, to end
> What my laborious life imagined, even
> The half imagined, the half written page.

Whatever their ultimate value, images themselves, acting on and in the imagination, bring us even to the kind of mood the Platonist would wish on us. For a moment the individual artist, longing for liberation of soul, succumbs to despair of this world and this life. We have to consider that "the half written page" is the poem we are reading: not yet complete and threatening to collapse from his despair and spiritual restlessness, yet obviously a poem he has found the will and means to finish. The despair is based on doubts about the worth or durability of his work as well as the temptation to renounce life. The "I" then lapses into the larger despair of the "we" who have been represented earlier:

> O but we dreamed to mend
> Whatever mischief seemed
> To afflict mankind, but now
> That winds of winter blow
> Learn that we were crack-pated when we dreamed.

The fourth section, like the second, compresses the historical meanings of the poem into a compact lyric. These lyric distillations are common to the working rhythms of *The Tower*, both within individual poems and from poem to poem. The compression is greater, the tone savage rather than wondering, and the rhetoric suggests a recapitulation of section 1 and a direct continuation of the discourse of section 3:

> IV
> We, who seven years ago
> Talked of honour and of truth,
> Shriek with pleasure if we show
> The weasel's twist, the weasel's tooth.

This is so emphatic a summary that it constitutes a kind of ending, but the poem continues, exploring its own labyrinth. Its continuation and its variations suggest that the knowledge of dissolution and historical regression, the aching consciousness of ephemerality, cannot destroy the creative impulse. Instead, the imagination presses back, coining epigrams, chasing images, and, in the fifth section, hammering out a sort of song:

> Come let us mock at the great
> That had such burdens on the mind
> And toiled so hard and late
> To leave some monument behind,
> Nor thought of the levelling wind.

The first line continues with variation in each stanza— "Come let us mock at the wise . . . Come let us mock at the good." Again, we must ask what group the pronoun includes. As earlier, it spreads out to include the educated classes in Ireland, the English, and all Europeans who chose to be bystanders and responded to change with cynicism and despair. But a clear subgroup must be artists, including the poet, who would not or could not make art serve the needs of civilization. The sense of "mimic" in "mock" comes into play here, so that we get an image of figures like Oscar Wilde, merchandising cynicism, of Ireland's treatment of her heroes and art-

ists, and finally of art's dangerous tendency simply to reflect
what is there. The very song making we are witness to
here becomes a self-defeating combination of derision and
imitation:

> Mock mockers after that
> That would not lift a hand maybe
> To help good, wise or great
> To bar that foul storm out, for we
> Traffic in mockery.

The verb "traffic" was used earlier for those who helped "in-
cendiary" and "bigot" destroy the Athenian heritage. The
"we" of the poem seems more and more to point specifically
to the artists who lived among the decay of their heritage
without fully acknowledging what was happening, or with-
out willingness to engage their art with the meanings of his-
torical change or the questioning of the myth of progress.

The final section of "Nineteen Hundred and Nineteen,"
like the final section of "Meditations in Time of Civil War,"
fills with visions of historical change, "phantoms of hatred
. . . and of the coming emptiness," brimming up into the
speaker's consciousness. In keeping with the impersonality of
"Nineteen Hundred and Nineteen," especially in relation to
the two poems that precede it, however, there is no rhetoric
of personality here—"I climb . . . I, my wits astray . . . I turn
away and shut the door"—to tincture the presentation of
what is seen. There are similar visionary moments in Yeats's
canon—one thinks of "The Valley of the Black Pig," "The
Cold Heaven," and "The Second Coming"—but this is the
most impersonal of them, the implication being that it does
not matter who is perceiving these visions; their "abstract
joy" and "half-read wisdom" are not the point. Historical
change has come to obliterate personality:

> Violence upon the roads: violence of horses;
> Some few have handsome riders, are garlanded
> On delicate sensitive ear or tossing mane,
> But wearied running round and round in their courses
> All break and vanish, and evil gathers head.

The guardsmen's drowsy chargers, the horses of a drunken sol-
diery, the nightmare, and some Irish folklore are here com-
pounded, as the poet's own note suggests:

The countrypeople see at times certain apparitions whom they
name now 'fallen angels,' now 'ancient inhabitants of the country,'
and describe as riding at whiles 'with flowers upon the head of the
horses.' I have assumed that these horsemen, now that the times
worsen, give way to worse.

As the poem has regrouped its scattered images of horses
and horsemen for an apocalyptic finale, it now does the same
with the images of dancers, labyrinth, and wind:

> Herodias' daughters have returned again
> A sudden blast of dusty wind and after
> Thunder of feet, tumult of images,
> Their purpose in the labyrinth of the wind;
> And should some crazy hand dare touch a daughter
> All turn with amorous cries, or angry cries,
> According to the wind, for all are blind.

Whitaker has documented the sources that Yeats brought to-
gether in these images, associating Salome with the Sidhe
(the wild host who rode the winds in Irish legend) and link-
ing both with deeply rooted mythologies of destructive
goddesses that go back to the Eumenides and of Dionysian
frenzies that combine love and anger, as in the story of the
Thracian women who dismembered Orpheus.[14] Again, Yeats

seems deliberately to have drawn his "tumult of images" from the nineties, from Symons and Wilde and the kind of subjects that Loie Fuller danced, here transformed into their truer meanings. Like the final section of "Meditations in Time of Civil War," this is a tripartite vision; when we compare the middle visions of both poems we get by contrast a bleaker vision in "Nineteen Hundred and Nineteen": the ladies on unicorns who muse in their sweetness and excess, "monstrous" but "familiar," are here displaced by creatures who match and intensify the first vision. The effect is extremely disquieting.

The third part of the vision gives us momentary hope when the winds of change seem to still for a moment; but they do so only to reveal individuals who bear the same kind of meaning as the horses and dancers:

> But now wind drops, dust settles; thereupon
> There lurches past, his great eyes without thought
> Under the shadow of stupid straw-pale locks,
> That insolent fiend Robert Artisson
> To whom the love-lorn Lady Kyteler brought
> Bronzed peacock feathers, red combs of her cocks.

Yeats has found a superb image around which to gather the meanings of his poem. The "ingenious lovely things" which the besotted Irish medieval aristocrat presses on her demon lover (whose name may have appealed to Yeats partly because of the pun it contained, bringing the makers of lovely things back into the poem once more by an astonishing route) take us back to the poem's beginning. The obviously fruitless relationship reminds us once more that "Man is in love and loves what vanishes." All that softens the horror of the image is Yeats's taking it from the distant past, a fact that he makes sure we understand in his note:

My last symbol, Robert Artisson, was an evil spirit much run after
in Kilkenny at the start of the fourteenth century. Are not those
who travel in the whirling dust also in the Platonic Year?

That last question deserves careful consideration. It im-
plies that those who personify destruction—the horses, the
daughters, the ironically named Artisson—are seen as part
of a larger cycle of change that is in fact orderly. But it is
orderly only by being recurrent. With her peacock feathers, a
favorite motif of art nouveau, Lady Kyteler sounds like a re-
cent contemporary of Yeats; being fourteenth century, she
gives us yet another reason to doubt the myth of progress.
The Robert Artissons and their lovelorn sponsors will come
and go, recede and return, a fact that is both comforting and
terrifying.

The placing of this great poem fourth in the sequence that
opens *The Tower* seems to me one of Yeats's most astute deci-
sions. It continues the retrenchment I have traced by giving
us the most relentless portrait of a world in which the de-
struction of civilized values and the objects which symbolize
them leaves the individual helpless and confused. But it does
this within an already established context of imaginative
success, even supremacy, so that it encourages us to balance
the *making* of "Nineteen Hundred and Nineteen"—the facts
of its very intricacy and beauty, along with its distance in
time as the earliest of the four poems we have read—against
the bleakness of its vision of destruction and change. By the
time we have faced the challenge of the first four poems in
this volume—as formidable a challenge as any poet ever set
his readers—we have an extremely satisfying sense of the
complex possibilities of interplay between the successful
imagination of the working artist and the forces of "real-
ity"—war, cycles of change, human perversity, the rhythmic
presence of creation and destruction in every life and every

civilization—against which it sets itself, torn between the desire to ignore and contradict, and the desire to accept and celebrate. When we take the "tired" image of the swan and find that it can thrill us yet once more, when we accept all the meanings of Artisson and Dame Kyteler and find Yeats's presentation of them "beautiful," we are not relapsing into the aestheticism of the nineties; we are balancing our acknowledgment that social progress (in Irish history and in the larger context of Western civilization) is a myth with our implicit understanding that Yeats's artistic progress is a triumphant reality.

5. Fabulous Darkness

Having taxed us with its formidable opening series, *The Tower* next relents a little with some shorter and easier poems. The three that follow "Nineteen Hundred and Nineteen"—"The Wheel," "Youth and Age," and "The New Faces" —are short (eight, four, and eight lines respectively) and relaxed in tone. They form a disparate chronological group (composed in 1921, 1924, and 1912) but are linked by their use of the perspective of old age—one of the book's themes— to offer insights into our experience of time and our relation to eternity. "The Wheel" suggests that our restlessness in desiring seasonal change conceals a "longing for the tomb," for oblivion and/or eternity. "Youth and Age" offers a familiar irony in concentrated form:

Much did I rage when young,
Being by the world oppressed,
But now with flattering tongue
It speeds the parting guest.

This matches the image of restlessness in the previous poem, but suggests that youth's fever can be supplanted both by a recognition of change and a fondness for its worldly manifestations. The poem can also be read as bitterly ironic at the expense of the world. In any case, the more personal note sounded by the shift from the "we" of "The Wheel" to the "I" of "Youth and Age" continues in "The New Faces," as the poet addresses a friend (Lady Gregory) who has grown old with him. Had she died, he would not care to revisit the places "Where we wrought that shall break the teeth of Time." The artistic vigor asserted here props up the conviction of the second quatrain:

> Let the new faces play what tricks they will
> In the old rooms; night can outbalance day,
> Our shadows roam the garden gravel still,
> The living seem more shadowy than they.

The victimization of age by time has through the course of the three poems undergone the kind of reversal performed in the poems that opened the volume. The shadows of the creators, representatives of the working imagination, have a vivid reality; on the "garden gravel" of at least one ancestral house, they defy time and change. The world may speed the parting guest, and longing for the tomb may underlie all that we do in this world, but Time's teeth can be broken now and then by the resistance of the accomplished work of art. The confidence sets the tone for the next poem, "A Prayer for My Son."

Those who compare this poem with its famous counterpart, "A Prayer for My Daughter," are apt to find it disappointing. It lacks the same scope and drama. It makes excellent sense, however, in its own right, especially by virtue of its place in *The Tower*. We can note first that the poem is not

meant to be very serious. It employs several exaggerations—
equating the normal parental desire that a new baby learn to
sleep through the night with the fear of plots of "devilish
things," a familiar address to God and Christ, an ordering up
of a "strong ghost" like a piece of household furniture—that
take their part in the more relaxed and playful mood of this
section of *The Tower*, and in its mingling of daily and domes-
tic concerns with large historical and mythic events. The
poem might be described as a redefinition of prayer. Its sum-
moning of a protective spirit ("Bid a strong ghost stand at the
head / That my Michael may sleep sound," and "Bid the ghost
have sword in fist"—with a glance at Michael's name) lacks
any hint of supplication. And the poet takes a familiar tone
with God, reminding Him of His humanity in the stories of
Christ's infancy:

> Though You can fashion everything
> From nothing every day, and teach
> The morning stars to sing,
> You have lacked articulate speech
> To tell Your simplest want, and know,
> Wailing upon a woman's knee,
> All of that worst ignominy
> Of flesh and bone;
>
> And when through all the town there ran
> The servants of Your enemy,
> A woman and a man,
> Unless the Holy Writings lie,
> Hurried through the smooth and rough
> And through the fertile and waste,
> Protecting, till the danger past,
> With human love.

Yeats almost seems to be lecturing God here, and we under-
stand that this new and peremptory form of prayer has be-

come possible in the context of *The Tower*, given the earlier claim that "man made up the whole." We also see, of course, that behind the rhetoric of appeal to the supernatural other purposes are at work. One is to establish a new dialectic, another rhythm of possibility, between absolute power and absolute helplessness. That confirms a growing sense that change and process are elements of the whole creation, not just of our lives and times. They affect even the creator. Another function of having the poet address his maker so familiarly is to confirm the poet as a master of the imagination. One creator is here addressing another.

The major emphasis of the poem, however, is its somewhat clumsy celebration of the value identified in its last two words, "human love." The story of God's infancy, which Yeats does not believe literally, touches him because of the way it bears on his own life, at the tower and in Dublin, with his young wife and two young children. His letters from this period are studded with tender and appreciative comments about his children and his wonder at the age-old images, now filling his own life, of nurture and infancy and growth. Some of the same concerns are reflected in the middle sections of "Meditations in Time of Civil War." I call Yeats's celebration of this "clumsy" in full recognition of the fact that he may have been conscious of the effect he was producing by formulating an elaborate and somewhat specious prayer to express the tenderness and protectiveness he felt for his son. It would be difficult to express the emotion directly without seeming trite, but it is also important that it be integrated with the world of *The Tower*, where personal emotions and impersonal insights revolve in a continual dance of opposition and partnership.

Having recalled Christ's birth, and having thus set up an interaction of the human and the divine, Yeats now begins to consider both divine and human, birth and death, in terms of large, repeating patterns of mythic change. His access to the "overculture" begins to be more frequent, less frightening. The emphasis of the volume has begun to shift from the contingencies of time and history—as represented by old age, civil war, and declining civilization—to the history of the imagination, its myths and artifacts. The stage was set for this new emphasis by "Nineteen Hundred and Nineteen," where the perspective on cyclically rising and falling civilizations allowed a recognition that there are dramatic points of crisis in the cycles; with that recognition came a consideration of the ways by which the imagination has portrayed such points of crisis. The shift of emphasis is completed and clarified in the diptych that comes next, "Two Songs from a Play."

The clarification, however, does not come cheap. Just when we thought the poems were growing easier, we find that an innocent-sounding title, which might lead us to expect a "Hey nonny nonny" or two, masks a ferociously condensed double lyric, huge in its implications and startling in its imaginative leaps. These are indeed songs that open and close Yeats's play, *The Resurrection*, but they are very far from the norm of songs in plays. The association with theater and the lyric formality of song help us shift from the domestic circumstances of the previous poem, but we are vaulted up to the visionary level that was attained gradually in "Nineteen Hundred and Nineteen" and "Meditations in Time of Civil War" with no more warning than the two simple words "I saw." These words form a misleadingly personal and mundane signal, given what follows:

I saw a staring virgin stand
Where holy Dionysus died,
And tear the heart out of his side,
And lay the heart upon her hand

And bear that beating heart away;
And then did all the Muses sing
Of Magnus Annus at the spring,
As though God's death were but a play.

What the speaker "saw" is quite extraordinary, already so in the first line because of the "staring virgin," a priestess or goddess. Her stare suggests blindness or a trance. Who is she? A daughter of Herodias? A musing Babylonian lady? Are her eyes, like Robert Artisson's, "great" and "without thought"? Is she caught up in events that subsume personality, ordinary awareness, and familiar use of the senses? Or is Yeats playing here on the Homeric epithet for Athena, gray-eyed, and her traditional association with the staring owl? Such meanings swirl around the adjective "staring," partly because of the way the poem's place in the volume sums them up.

The virgin performs a hideous ritual, but it produces a chorus of praise that in turn triggers the speaker's reaction, "As though God's death were but a play." Is it the fact of singing, or the content of the song that produces this reaction? A chorus of muses certainly suggests the theater, but their affirmation of huge historical cycles that are as natural as the seasonal changes might also produce a sense of theatricality because "God's death" in such cycles is part of a pattern or plot and no more a real death than that of a tragic hero on the stage. The word "play" also carries its additional senses of "fun" and "illusion." The invocation of *homo ludens* in the double perspective of annual renewal and gigantic historical cycle is intentional and exhilarating. The largest elements of reality are a kind of theater of metaphysics.

The second stanza confirms the insight by setting myths and historical cycles side by side. If the song is sung, as Yeats's note tells us, at the occasion of "Christ's first appearance to the Apostles after the Resurrection," then it combines historical retrospection—a witnessing of a death and rebirth ritual from the old Dionysian religion—with prediction, a recognition that the events of the classical world will repeat themselves in the history of Christianity:

Another Troy must rise and set,
Another lineage feed the crow,
Another Argo's painted prow
Drive to a flashier bauble yet.
The Roman Empire stood appalled:
It dropped the reins of peace and war
When that fierce virgin and her Star
Out of the fabulous darkness called.

The perspective that takes in two-thousand-year cycles as calmly as we do the change of seasons is lofty and playful. It uses metonymies—"feed the crow" for all the deaths in battle of the Trojan War, "dropped the reins" for the decline and fall of the Roman Empire—and sums up whole epics in single phrases, some of them rather slangy, as when the Golden Fleece becomes a flashy bauble. To portray a great empire as an awestruck charioteer is to free us from the immediacy of suffering and historical change as presented in poems like "Meditations in Time of Civil War." When we get far enough back from the fact of change we lose detail but gain tranquillity, seeing the rise and fall of whole civilizations as a pageant staged to entertain us.

The most remarkable connection that the first song makes, of course, involves the two virgins. The first is a pagan priestess or goddess, involved in a savage ritual. The second is Mary, whose traditional attributes of gentleness and mercy are now displaced by her ferocity and proprietary association with the Christmas Star. The transformation reminds us, as "The Second Coming" did, that great beginnings do not exist without great endings, that the onset of Christianity was the death of something else, so that Mary's role cannot be other than "fierce." At the same time, her ferocity is qualified, like everything else, by the artifice and theatricality. In a song from a play we are hearing about an experience and set of insights that seemed theatrical to their witness. We're at a safe distance.

The second song elaborates these insights. Its first stanza, which was all there was of it in the original edition of *The Tower*, concentrates on the birth, life, and death of Christ:

> In pity for man's darkening thought
> He walked that room and issued thence
> In Galilean turbulence;
> The Babylonian Starlight brought
> A fabulous, formless darkness in;
> Odour of blood when Christ was slain
> Made Plato's tolerance in vain
> And vain the Doric discipline.

Again, the compression Yeats achieves here is nothing short of astonishing. "He walked that room" is typical, suggesting as it does through very ordinary diction Mary's womb, the tomb from which Christ rose, human life, human thought, and simple architecture. Yeats, or his singer, insists on balance throughout the stanza. The advent of Christianity, traditionally viewed as human progress, destroys Platonic tolerance and Doric discipline. The newness of it all, "Galilean turbulence," has its secret relation to the old, "Babylonian Starlight," which helped produce it. And the "fabulous darkness" out of which Mary called in the first song recurs, with a second attribute: it is also "formless," breaking old forms down and making new forms possible.

A realm of mystery, then, where we cannot see the origins of the startling events that shape our history and civilizations, is the source of all this energy and change, and the poet/singer has twice been able to point to it. In 1931 Yeats wrote and added the stanza that not only gave the two songs formal symmetry but connected this poem more firmly to the insights of "Nineteen Hundred and Nineteen" ("Man is in love and loves what vanishes") and of "The Tower" ("man made up the whole, / Made lock, stock and barrel / Out of his bitter soul"):

Everything that man esteems
Endures a moment or a day.
Love's pleasure drives his love away,
The painter's brush consumes his dreams,
The herald's cry, the soldier's tread
Exhaust his glory and his might:
Whatever flames upon the night
Man's own resinous heart has fed.

As the poem moves from the beating heart of God to the resinous human heart, the tone grows more complex. We have been able to contemplate gigantic cycles of historical change with equanimity, even enjoyment. Now we are asked to remember that the human relation to these matters continues to be problematic and agonizing. Humans make it all up and fuel it, but cannot accept its ephemerality or the interlocking of rise and fall, energy and exhaustion. The "fabulous, formless darkness" is finally our own "darkening thought," but we cannot retain that insight, and our dreams continue to drive us on, as the fires fed by our hearts flame gloriously against the night.

The attitudes of sections 2 and 3 of "Nineteen Hundred and Nineteen" are very much present in "Two Songs from a Play." The manner, however, is more compressed and lyrical. As in "The Wheel," Yeats is able to combine great scope with great concentration because he can rely on ideas and images that the longer poems have offered us. If we have attended to those insights, we can negotiate the metonymic manner and summarizing gestures now before us. And we can deal next with an even more compressed example, called "Fragments."[15]

Like "Two Songs," this poem is a diptych, two matched segments, though its title suggests formal uncertainty. In fact, the imagination's ability to transform, compare, and revivify its myths is nowhere more confidently asserted:

> I
> Locke sank into a swoon;
> The Garden died;
> God took the spinning-jenny
> Out of his side.

The onset of materialism and the industrial revolution is a parody of the creation and fall of man. Specifically, his new helpmeet is to be a machine. The cyclical versions of history are here treated less seriously and the handling of myth is more witty and irreverent. Having presented us with such imaginative extravagance in four lines, the poet anticipates our response:

> II
> Where got I that truth?
> Out of a medium's mouth,
> Out of nothing it came,
> Out of the forest loam,
> Out of dark night where lay
> The crowns of Ninevah.

The reader who has trouble understanding why there can be four answers to the question is best directed to the concluding lines of "Two Songs," where the equating is more explicit.

The two poems mirror and gloss each other, and Yeats's decision, when he wrote "Fragments," about where to place it was surely the right one. As for its title, that seems in part an acknowledgment of the poet's way of assembling his images into mosaics that retain their disparate character even as they form larger wholes. It is also an image of the modern world.

"Wisdom" gives further consideration to *The Tower*'s preoccupation with the ways that imagination acts upon reality in making art. Art is synthesis, as we have seen, when civilizations and religions and moments of historical change are brought together, and as this poem further suggests by tracing Christ's transformation, at the hands of artists, from carpenter's son, to miracle-worker, to personification of divine and human wisdom. In the artist's hands the love of fine things—"painted panel, statuary, / Glass-mosaic, window-glass"—tames and modifies mystery:

> Miracle had its playtime where
> In damask clothed and on a seat
> Chryselephantine, cedar boarded,
> His majestic Mother sat
> Stitching at a purple hoarded,
> That He might be nobly breeched,
> In starry towers of Babylon
> Noah's freshet never reached.

In the process of adjusting to momentous change, this poem reminds us, we try to ignore its disquieting origins, the "fabulous, formless darkness" it springs from. The poem gently mocks "the true faith" and its self-deceptions. The sawdust on the carpenter's floor is swept away by idealizing, and the god's "wild infancy" that paradoxically "Drove horror from His Mother's breast" is lost sight of when his "cognomen" becomes "Wisdom."

A comparable vitiation can overcome art when it loses touch with its origins. Yeats has in mind here the early Christian elaborations of sacred imagery in "painted panel, statuary, / Glass-mosaic, window-glass," and Mary on a chryselephantine seat "Stitching at a purple," but he is also commenting implicitly on symbolism's confidence, at one extreme, that art could separate itself from experience and be a perfected realm complete in itself. The rhythms of creation and destruction seen in history are essential to the workings of imagination; myth must return periodically to its savage origins and art must return to the forest loam, or to what Yeats would later characterize as the "foul rag-and-bone shop of the heart."

These insights help explain how it is that Yeats can periodically rise above his multiple cultural commitments, that is, how his artistic freedom comes about; it is because he sees process as essential to creation. To be encumbered by experience and entangled in history is to accept and enter a rhythm that will reward the artistic imagination with vigor and independence. It is climbing on the wheel at the bottom in order to ride it to the top. It is Yeats's modification of symbolist austerity, the modernist perspective that furnishes the essential medium and unique structure of *The Tower*.

"Wisdom" shows too how effective the book's context can become for individual poems. By itself it would seem rather peculiar and incomplete. As part of its sequence, especially the group of poems discussed in this chapter, it takes its place in a continuing meditation on art, imagination, myth, and the human endeavor to know the unknowable.

6. Swan and Centaur

In the careful ordering of *The Tower*, at a midway point, comes Yeats's great sonnet "Leda and the Swan." The poem's placement is superb. Its succinctness and power would be striking in any context, but at the center of *The Tower* it functions as a kind of icon, a magical illustration of the volume's many themes, drawing into its language and imagery the surging energies and incessant oppositions by which Yeats has characterized reality. It is a poem about the way a moment of crisis can be understood when seen as part of a larger pattern; as a poem carefully placed in the comprehensive design of *The Tower*, it acts out its truth, becoming an emblem of its own meaning.

The poem reflects, once more, Yeats's mixed cultural allegiances. Outside *The Tower* it might seem to have little or nothing to do with Ireland, but in the context of the volume its violence epitomizes the torn and frightening world of recent Irish history. I do not mean of course that Zeus personifies England and helpless Leda Ireland, but rather that suffering and violence as manifestations of historical change are by this point in *The Tower* associated with Ireland when they are presented with immediacy. And "Leda and the Swan," from the first moment ("A sudden blow") is nothing if not immediate in its use of violence.

As a sonnet, of course, the poem connects with a literary tradition, manifested through English poetry, that Yeats was unwilling to reject, either as part of his nationalism or as a definition of his modernism. The argument about how violently modern art must repudiate its own traditions had been raging for some time, among all the "isms": cubism, futurism, imagism, vorticism, surrealism. Yeats's own answer, evident everywhere in *The Tower*, is superbly summed up by "Leda and the Swan." As a sonnet, it confirms a continuity with tradition. At the same time, as a sonnet unlike any other in the language, its newness and modernity are unmistakable. It transforms tradition as radically as other modernist masterpieces.

The poem's connection with the turn-of-the-century values of symbolism is equally evident. It retells a myth in somewhat decadent terms, and it feels uncompromising and confrontational—not as difficult as, say, a poem by Mallarmé, but much more in that vein than resembling typical Irish or Georgian English poems of the period. Then too, of course, it features that favorite symbolist image, a swan. We have already seen Yeats reconstituting this emblem to stand for the poet facing mortality in "The Tower" and the human soul mirrored in all its tragic stateliness in "Nineteen Hundred and Nineteen." Now he transforms it into godhead, raping a helpless victim, an image of terrifying and overpowering mystery. Readers of *The Tower* may have been prepared to see the image used again, but not in this startling guise. It reminds us how freely the collection handles its own recurring symbols, pitching them into the world of process and dialectic.

"Leda and the Swan" draws on themes articulated in the series of shorter poems treated in the previous chapter, illustrating and qualifying their meanings. The contrast of absolute power and absolute helplessness that characterized God's history in "A Prayer for My Son" is now, perhaps more properly, a divine-human opposition, so that the more comfortable interactions of God and man in "A Prayer for My Son" and "Two Songs from a Play" turn into a confrontation that stresses all the differences, real and imagined, between the immortal and the mortal. The metonymic treatment of rising and falling civilizations and of whole epics characteristic of "Two Songs" finds its counterpart here in the characterization of an orgasm: "A shudder in the loins engenders there / The broken wall, the burning roof and tower / And Agamemnon dead." And the need for art and religion to return to the primitive energy of their origins, discussed but not illustrated in "Wisdom," is here convincingly demonstrated, as both myth and art are startlingly reborn. It is as though we really are present at events in the "fabulous darkness" that "Two Songs" and "Fragments" could only point to. Yeats is making good on his own aesthetic claims.

We know that "Leda and the Swan" envisions a moment with vast implications—the engendering of Helen, who will bring two civilizations to their confrontation and separate crises; we know that it is thus a powerful emblem for the way larger forces—history, natural and supernatural patterns of change—can dominate and victimize an individual consciousness. We know these things if we have been reading carefully through *The Tower*, for they have been among its foremost concerns, in the formidable opening sequence of four poems as well as the subsequent six that lead up to "Leda."

What we also know is what it means at this moment to be Leda: the sudden blow, the webs caressing the thighs, the bill holding the nape of the neck, the "vague fingers" pushing helplessly at what is moving between her "loosening thighs," and, finally, the shudder that is the swan's at orgasm and perhaps also hers, in involuntary response. The poem is remarkable, in other words, for its simultaneity: a concentration of the physical and immediate sensations of the rape, with their accompanying terror and incomprehension, and at the same time a detached understanding of the meaning of all this, as history and as myth.

Other commentators help us see that the best way to misread a poem is to take it too literally. That is what Yvor Winters did with this (and many another) poem: he chose to think that Yeats believed it literally and that unless the reader could do that too the poem would not work.[16] He was wrong, on both counts. Harold Bloom, who cites Winters, tends to follow suit: "I wish though that the Yeats sonnet had just a touch of the Shelleyan skepticism about divine power and knowledge."[17] Winters wishes Yeats were a neoclassical rationalist; Bloom wishes he were an early romantic, Blake or Shelley, and in the process does not see the skeptical humanism that pervades *The Tower* and this poem as well.

Readers less encumbered by preconceptions will have less difficulty with "Leda and the Swan." They will recognize that it is not only a dramatic reenactment of myth, but about myth, and, more specifically, about the implications of determinism in mythology. The two questions in the octave—

How can those terrified vague fingers push
The feathered glory from her loosening thighs?
And how can body, laid in that white rush
But feel the strange heart beating where it lies?

—speak not only to Leda's emotions, but to the pressures and terrors of history as Yeats has been exploring them in *The Tower*. Another commentator, Robert Snukal, sums it up as follows:

Leda is being raped, not only by a god, but by history as a god. . . . The shudder in her loins "engenders" the destruction of Troy. But all this happens to her; it catches her by surprise and is inflicted on her. It is the utter subjugation of the individual to history conceived as a determined flow of events that is described in the octave.[18]

So far, so good. But the poem is a sonnet, and it takes a sonnet's characteristic turn, so that the third question it poses (drawing out implications from the second) takes us to different considerations:

> Being so caught up,
> So mastered by the brute blood of the air,
> Did she put on his knowledge with his power
> Before the indifferent beak could let her drop?

Snukal feels that this is more of the same:

The effect of the final question is to drive home the power and irrationality of history, of what is indifferent and beyond humanity, and to reinforce our sense of helplessness and confusion in the face of so much power. . . . What Yeats finds terrifying is not the facts of mutability and change, but the possibility that the process of life may be utterly beyond human control, that history might be the result of something other than human consciousness.[19]

This seems to me a refusal, like Bloom's and Winters's, to stand outside the myth, as myth. The source of "Leda and the Swan" is not history, not what we call "fact," but the human imagination, nothing other than "human consciousness," which produced it as a kind of speculative artifact, an emblem powerful enough to continue to appeal to painters, sculptors, and poets. By ending with a question, Yeats points to the imaginative speculation inherent in the myth. Who has the knowledge, and who has the power?

The power itself seems to be shared. Yeats might have said "and" or "or" where he says "with": the human takes on some of the power of the divine through this sexual encounter, this crossbreeding of omnipotence and helplessness. And the knowledge? The very existence of the myth is paradoxical: its story says that Leda cannot grasp the implications of what is happening to her, but the myth itself—understood by Yeats as human in origin—*is* the knowledge, purporting to know as the god knows, offering to explain history, humanity, and divinity. Yeats has created a poem so powerful that its commentators feel he must somehow be a helpless part of it— ignorant, confused, credulous. To have made the poem, however, is to have transformed myth to metaphor, to be both inside and outside of myth, involved and detached. We compare the beating heart of the god here—how could she help "But feel" it—with the beating heart of Dionysus in "Two Songs from a Play," and we remember that both are a projection of "man's own resinous heart." There is helpless Leda, there is all-powerful Zeus controlling her, and beyond Zeus there is Yeats, the mythographer, controlling him in turn. And beyond Yeats? The whole rhetoric of questioning to which the poem resorts should help us keep such questions open. We are after all reading a book of poems, *The Tower*, where the consideration of human imaginings about determinism and freedom is a constant topic, an issue unsettled.

The curious and little-known companion piece to "Leda and the Swan" is a poem of almost the same length (sixteen lines) with a relatively elaborate title: "On a Picture of a

Black Centaur by Edmund Dulac." It is another poem that could be called iconic—the centaur seems to be a representative of the fabulous darkness and daemonic images Yeats has been treating through the course of *The Tower*—but we are also struck by differences from the Leda poem: the tone is more contemplative, the poem deals with a work of art rather than a revivified myth, a living artist is named in the title, and the speaker is altogether more personal, the Yeatsian persona from earlier pieces like "The Tower" and "Meditations in Time of Civil War." Still, the encounter with the myth in the Leda poem and the contemplation of the pictured mythic creature in this poem are an interesting sequence. Artists have so often chosen Leda and the swan as a subject that the gap between the Leda sonnet and a poem about a picture of a centaur is not as great as it might at first seem.

Yeats opens the poem by addressing the centaur directly, claiming a sort of relationship:

> Your hooves have stamped at the black margin of the wood,
> Even where horrible green parrots call and swing.
> My works are all stamped down into the sultry mud.
> I knew that horse play, knew it for a murderous thing.

A double creature, the centaur seems to be able to come and go between the mythic world of fabulous darkness and the familiar world of daylight reality with relative ease. The wood is not a surprising symbol for the darker and more remote world; it will turn up in the "Oedipus at Colonus" poems later in the volume. The parrots are a bit more startling. Yeats's fondness for birds as representatives of the spiritual and numinous gives them a context; even so, they make an exotic addition to the parade of swans, peacocks, owls, stares, hawks, daws, moorhens, and Grecian goldsmiths' handiwork we have seen so far in *The Tower*. They lend a tropical suggestion to the proceedings and a strong effect to the color scheme.

The speaker, "Yeats" once more, is discouraged about his own poetry, which he sees as stamped down into the mud. Has the centaur done the stamping? I think not. The contrast seems to be between the "horse-play" that comes naturally to a mythic being who can stamp and the "murderous" effect it can have on a mortal, who is more likely to be stamped than to stamp, or, as in this case, to have his "works" stamped down by misapprehending readers and critics. In other words, the contrast between the mythical, supernatural, and immortal beings on the one hand and helpless humans on the other—a contrast exploited in "Leda" and shortly to be investigated in "Among School Children"—is maintained here. The speaker-poet knows the world that the centaur knows, but knows too that his contacts with it have been far more costly. He goes on to a review of his artistic activities, which have apparently involved him too deeply in the occult world of spiritual mysteries:

> What wholesome sun has ripened is wholesome food to eat,
> And that alone; yet I, being driven half insane
> Because of some green wing, gathered old mummy wheat
> In the mad abstract dark and ground it grain by grain
> And after baked it slowly in an oven.

Now we find out why the speaker considers the parrots horrible. They have somehow drawn him into the "mad abstract dark" and led him into a foolish enterprise: gathering wheat that has lain for centuries in crypts and tombs, to grind and bake it. In other words, all his effort may simply have led to something inedible and unwholesome, anything but the "daily bread" poetry should aspire to be, and a dreadful distortion of communion as well.

That Yeats has holy communion in mind is confirmed by the fact that he now brings wine into the poem. As he does so, the mood begins to shift (this poem turns at its halfway point, unlike a sonnet) and the artistic confidence returns. The poet has not reformed, being still deeply preoccupied with ancient and occult items of diet, but since wine is supposed to improve with age, that part of his offering is positive:

> . . . but now
> I bring full flavoured wine out of a barrel found
> Where seven Ephesian topers slept and never knew
> When Alexander's empire past, they slept so sound.

Half his communion is successful; that, along with his being "half insane," gives him more kinship with the half-and-half centaur than he seemed to have at first. By now he has grown so confident that he can offer to take over the centaur's apparent task of keeping watch on the wood's margin and the parrots:

> Stretch out your limbs and sleep a long Saturnian sleep;
> I have loved you better than my soul for all my words,
> And there is none so fit to keep a watch and keep
> Unwearied eyes upon those horrible green birds.

Instead of Leda raped by Zeus, we have a declaration of love here. Yeats will serve his wine, a potent soporific, to the centaur, then keep the watch himself. It is hard to be sure who is "so fit," given the syntax, but I take it to be the speaker, arguing his qualifications to replace the centaur as sentinel. The "unwearied eyes" he claims to have connect to the references to eyes as instruments of special power—seers, visionaries, staring virgins, hawks, and fiends—that have recurred so frequently in *The Tower*.

The fact that the poem is addressed not to a centaur but to the image of a centaur in a painting by a modern illustrator makes the whole situation more complex. What makes it even stranger is the possibility, detailed in an account of the writing of the poem by Cecil Salkeld and quoted at length in Hone's biography of Yeats, that the picture wasn't by Dulac at all, but by Salkeld. In this anecdote, one of the most fascinating pictures of Yeats at work on a poem we have been given, Salkeld painted a picture of a centaur after an afternoon of walking and talking with Yeats about various matters, and in the morning Yeats presented him with the poem.[20]

Assuming that Salkeld's account is basically true, we have to ask why Yeats changed Salkeld to Dulac in the title. No painting of a black centaur by Dulac has turned up, and it's quite possible that Yeats enjoyed the joke of writing about an imaginary painting. On the other hand, Dulac wasn't chosen casually. He was friendly with Yeats and was designing materials for the tower at Ballylee, such as a bedspread with the centaur motif, a symbol Dulac was fond of and that Yeats obviously liked too.[21] For any reader of the period, too, Dulac's name would evoke a well-known illustrator who customarily dealt with fantasy and magic. It was rather like saying "a fairy by Arthur Rackham." Dulac's imaginative freedom, which led him to respond not so much to nature as to myth, fantasy, and the visualizing of psychological and hallucinatory states, appealed enormously to Yeats. Writing about a composite animal, Yeats may well have smiled as he created a composite picture, half Dulac's and half Salkeld's, and presented himself as a composite artist, half failure and half success, half insane and half wise, with a composite communion, half-inedible (half-baked?) mummy bread and half-"full-flavoured" wine.

"On a Picture of a Black Centaur by Edmund Dulac," then, takes its place among the other declarations of artistic inde-

pendence and confidence in *The Tower*. The poet criticizes
his own tendency to abstraction and the occult, comes to
terms with it, and argues that his new poems represent a sig-
nificant advance. If we want immediate evidence for Yeats's
confidence about having something special to offer, we can
look at the poems on either side. In "Leda and the Swan," for
example, Yeats did seem to succeed in breaking the teeth of
time. From an incredible distance he brought a story, a group
of images, whose meaning and intensity he was able to pre-
sent with unusual vividness and immediacy. Time's relativity
was apparently much on Yeats's mind when he was writing
"Centaur." He said to Salkeld on their walk:

"Do you realize that eternity is not a long time but a short time
. . . ?" I just said, I didn't quite understand. "Eternity," Yeats said,
"Eternity is in the glitter on the beetle's wing . . . it is something
infinitely short. . . ." I said that I could well conceive "infinity"
being excessively small as well as being excessively large. "Yes,"
he said, apparently irrelevantly, "I was thinking of those Ephesian
topers." [22]

Time's elasticity, as experienced by the Ephesian "topers,"
can be very apparent to a poet as he contemplates the time-
lessness, the new-old quality, of his images. He makes a new
combination—e.g., Locke, God, Adam, and the spinning
jenny—and then says that it came out of the distant past
("dark night where lay / The crowns of Ninevah"), as well as
"out of nowhere." Old wine in new barrels? A wink of eter-
nity? When one spends a lot of time in the mad, abstract
dark, gathering mummy wheat, it gets hard to explain things
to the Cecil Salkelds, and you find yourself talking to cen-
taurs. Daemonic images, as *The Tower* has more than once
demonstrated, are sometimes the only company the poet has,
and in talking to them we can never be sure we aren't really

addressing ourselves. In writing this poem I think Yeats meant to relax the atmosphere of *The Tower* a little, to tease himself about his own preoccupations: the "full flavoured wine" may well stand for some of the materials he was excited about getting for *A Vision*, by means of automatic writing, through his wife. The problem is that the poem is a little too obscure for most readers, with the result that its genial humor and self-deprecation do not come across as readily as Yeats might have liked.

7. The Long Schoolroom

This chapter will be devoted to "Among School Children," one of Yeats's finest poems. My argument, sometimes explicit, more often implicit, will be that its greatness stems in part from its careful placement in *The Tower*, and that it can be best understood when examined in that context. What follows will strike a balance. "Among School Children" would be a huge success in any context; its placement in the second half of *The Tower* enhances both the poem and the volume's design.

It gives, for one thing, a sense of beginning all over again, a relatively welcome perception in a poet whose sense of reality is dominated by the cyclic and whose perception of order in a chaotic world comes from recurrence and renewal. We are once more in Ireland, once more with the aging, beset speaker of "Sailing to Byzantium" and "The Tower," the elderly poet whose strength of imagination is both a curse and a blessing. The mention of school in the title and first line recalls the "singing school" that studied "monuments of its own magnificence" in "Sailing to Byzantium" and the speaker's resolve to "make my soul / Compelling it to study / In a learned school" in "The Tower." Our curiosity is piqued by the implicit drama of recurrence: is this a relapse of the kind we experienced in moving from "Sailing to Byzantium" to "The Tower," or is it a triumphant recasting of the problems treated early in the book, this time in a less equivocal fashion?

Part of the poem's drama, aside from its echoes of the opening of *The Tower*, stems from the conflicting cultural affinities discussed earlier as a problem that Yeats converts into a strength by his willingness to dramatize it. Here we see him as an Irish senator, a "sixty year old smiling public man" touring a model elementary school in the young Republic, more trapped in his role as an Irish nationalist than we have so far seen him. The disjunction between inner man, full of memories and beset by his wild imagination, and the outer public role, a kind of scarecrow in his own sense of himself, is sharper here than at any point in *The Tower*, and the sense of transformation from "On a Picture of a Black Centaur by Edmund Dulac," where the speaker felt free to pursue a dreamy meditation, addressing an imaginary creature without fear of interruption, is especially acute.

At the same time, we are reminded of Yeats's ties to the traditions of English poetry by his return here to the ottava rima stanza derived from Byron, used earlier in "Sailing to Byzantium" and the first section of "Nineteen Hundred and Nineteen." A poem of eight eight-line stanzas with an intricate and pleasing rhyme scheme is obviously, at least in one sense, a very traditional affair, not necessarily Irish and certainly not necessarily modern.

Yet European modernism makes itself felt in the poem, not only through the desire for an art that is perfect and independent, but through the school Senator Yeats is visiting as well, a school modeled on European attempts at pedagogical reform at the turn of the century. This one is based on the ideals of Maria Montessori, who opened her first Casa dei Bambini in Rome in 1907. When Yeats says that the children "learn to cipher and to sing, / To study reading-books and history, / To cut and sew, be neat in everything / In the best modern way," he is being quite literal: their activities reflect the idealism of turn-of-the-century Europe, the world that believed so firmly in progress and human betterment and that was so violently fractured by the First World War. The importation of that world and its educational ideals to Ireland in the 1920s is something Yeats cannot help feeling equivocal about. He recognizes its value at the same time that he sees its limitations and naiveté, and "the best modern way" inevitably has an ironic flavor. The setting also makes plausible the speaker's sudden memories of his own days of youthful idealism, which belong to that lost world and survive to the present only in ambiguous form.

For all the complex associations one can discern behind the poem even before one is very far into it, its strength lies in its simplicity and directness. The first line is such a notable example of this quality that we do well to pause and admire it before taking up the poem's unfolding drama:

I walk through the long schoolroom questioning,

This gives us the poem's setting with admirable succinctness. If it also begins to fill with echoes and associations, that is partly because of the poet's careful choice of diction (try substituting "around" for "through" or "large" for "long") and partly from the associations that crowd in from earlier poems in *The Tower*. I have already touched on the "school" associations that recall the volume's opening poems. "Walk" is similarly charged, recalling the many meanings that "he walked that room" summoned to itself in "Two Songs from a Play." "Questioning" is a process we have seen explicitly treated—"As I would question all, come all who can" in "The Tower"—and implicitly present in poem after poem in the form of questions that reflect the speaker's uncertainty or the difficulty of resolving issues the poems have raised. In fact, *The Tower* has tended to oscillate between assertive phases—marked by a rhetoric of confident declaration, and skeptical passages, marked by a rhetoric of questioning—and we will see that very oscillation in "Among School Children."

Even the word "long," the adjective for the large, open Montessori-style classroom, has its curious echoes of earlier moments in *The Tower*: "a long / Last reach of glittering stream" where the swan floats out to sing its last song, and a chorus that commends "all summer long" a world of incessant change. In short, we can see the poem's opening line simultaneously as naturalistic reporting and as existential declaration, where the long schoolroom becomes a metaphor for life's uncertainties; we do this partly because *The Tower* has trained us, through example and association, to look for such simultaneity.

As the first stanza unfolds, then, we are both inside and outside, like the speaker, present in the classroom observing the children but seeing in their activities—even their cutting and sewing—reflections of the poet's life, world, and sensibility as demonstrated in earlier poems. For the children it is innocent and well-planned education. For the poet and for readers who have come to this point with him, there are issues of birth and death, of the human struggle to make sense of time, of the threat of chaos posed by war and historical change, of the effort of art to tell the truth and offer solace at the same time. At the close of the first stanza, using the now-familiar images of eyes and staring, the speaker sees the children seeing him:

> . . . the children's eyes
> In momentary wonder stare upon
> A sixty year old smiling public man.

The self-consciousness of this is also testimony to the activity behind the facade of "smiling public man" of that "Excited, passionate, fantastical imagination" of "The Tower" and other poems, so that we need feel no surprise when the second stanza opens with "I dream," another deceptively simple formulation. The speaker is being visited by images from the past. One means by which Yeats expresses ambivalence about his strong imagination in this and other volumes is through contrasts between moments when images come like summoned spirits at the poet-conjuror's bidding, and moments when they haunt or assault him without warning. Such tensions inhabit this poem as effectively as at any other moment in the whole Yeats canon. When the poet says "I dream," we suspect that he may not do so by preference, but that as soon as the image/memory of a youthful moment of unity with Maud Gonne arrives, he dwells on it lovingly. This leads him, however, to look at the children and "wonder" about her when she was even younger than when he first knew her. She might have been homely or ungainly like some of these children, since "daughters of the swan"—through the familiar story of the ugly duckling and through the fact that all "paddlers" have their ungainly moments—can be awkward too. The fact that she might have resembled these children rather than her later, Helen-like self brings beauty and plainness, daydream and reality, together with a dramatic jolt, the unforgettable close of the third stanza:

And thereupon my heart is driven wild:
She stands before me as a living child.

The effect is unwelcome and involuntary, and it stresses the vulnerability of the old man, whose habit of distilling "the half-read wisdom of daemonic images" can lead to such sudden assaults in inappropriate circumstances. We note, however, that the smiling public man can maintain his facade, masking his wild heart and in the process reflecting the poet who stands outside the poem and achieves the detachment necessary to cast it into rhyme and meter. The Yeats who is helpless to control his imagination, memory or emotions, is balanced by the Yeats who has managed a cool dramatization of that helplessness in finely tuned ottava rima stanzas. The balancing of tensions that will close the poem is already before us.

The next "visitation" is milder—"Her present image floats into the mind"—but the poem's first half concludes with the poet still in confusion about the disparity between his inward state and outward appearance, his vivid imaginings and drab, constrained role. Again, the images—Leda, birds, smile, scarecrow—evolve from the vocabulary and iconography of *The Tower*:

And I though never of Ledaean kind
Had pretty plumage once—enough of that,
Better to smile on all that smile, and show
There is a comfortable kind of old scarecrow.

After this point, the poem does not return to the "real" schoolroom situation, but evolves steadily as a meditation on the power of images as against the power of change. The distressed persona is transformed into a speaker whose merging with the maker of the poem is one part of our satisfaction with its progress. The "sixty year old smiling public man," haunted by memories and imaginings, evolves into the defiant, exultant speaker of the poem's close. In a sense he was the shell from which the poem was to hatch, no less important for that function. In providing a base and a rhetoric from which the poem can launch itself, he approximates the relation between artist and work of art. Again, we realize, Yeats is giving us a poetry that deals in its own beginnings and becomings. Behind the apparently casual use of association, drifting thought, and backing into insight, is an expert and symmetrical design that is the more pleasing for our gradual recognition of it.[23]

The second half of "Among School Children" provides us with a panorama of images, image-worshippers, and image-makers. The gallery is drawn from other poems in *The Tower* in such a way as to make us feel that we are witnessing a climax or apogee. The "youthful mother" of stanza five, for example, recalls the mother birds of "The Tower" and "Meditations," the murdered mother of "Nineteen Hundred and Nineteen," the mother of his own child in "A Prayer for My Son," Mary as invoked in "Two Songs from a Play" and "Wisdom" (one reason for preferring its earlier placement), and of course Leda. The world the poet has been grappling with throughout the volume, the world where everything "is begotten, born and dies" here converges on the mother and child, victimized by the "honey of generation" and trapped, like the artist, in the problem of reconciling the real and the ideal:

> What youthful mother, a shape upon her lap
> Honey of generation had betrayed,
> And that must sleep, shriek, struggle to escape
> As recollection or the drug decide,
> Would think her son, did she but see that shape

With sixty or more winters on its head,
A compensation for the pang of his birth,
Or the uncertainty of his setting forth?

Mother and child are familiar characters to the reader of
The Tower; so is Plato, who nevertheless startles us a bit—
Yeats's transitions in this poem can be quite abrupt—by
opening stanza six. We recall that the speaker of "The Tower"
talked first of choosing Plato for a friend, then turned on him
in an antimetaphysical reaction, crying "in Plato's teeth."
Plato gave his name both to the Platonic year of "Nineteen
Hundred and Nineteen" and the Platonic tolerance made vain
in "Two Songs from a Play." His followers were present too, in
the Platonist of *Il Penseroso*, who toiled late in "Meditations"
and the Platonist in "Nineteen Hundred and Nineteen," who
affirmed the need to "cast off body and trade." Plato draws on
earlier associations, then, but what is he doing here? For one
thing, like the speaker, like all mortals, including other phi-
losophers, he is a mother's child:

> Plato thought nature but a spume that plays
> Upon a ghostly paradigm of things;
> Solider Aristotle played the taws
> Upon the bottom of a king of kings;
> World-famous golden-thighed Pythagoras
> Fingered upon a fiddle-stick or strings
> What a star sang and careless Muses heard:
> Old clothes upon old sticks to scare a bird.

Once again Yeats has brought together apparent opposites.
Mother and child were both at the mercy of their imagina-
tions. She needed to idealize her child in order to make preg-
nancy and the pain and trouble of childrearing worthwhile,
while the child might or might not succeed in "recollecting"

its prenatal freedom, fitfully if at all.[24] But the sages, whom he had asked to welcome him into the holy fire of Byzantium, were exemplars of human wisdom and lasting achievement. Surely they were less tormented by the discrepancy between imagination and reality than the public man or the mother and child? In fact, Plato, Aristotle, and Pythagoras—doubting, spanking, fiddling—had mothers of their own, and grew to be scarecrows too, made ridiculous by their subjection to old age through time. The Muses (who chorused in "Two Songs" and one of whom was to be bid to "go pack" in "The Tower") can be "careless" as they listen to the heavenly music Pythagoras captures; he is not free of care, and his efforts will wear him out.

Apparently existence disappoints either through the failure of the real to approximate the ideal, as with the mothers, or the failure of the ideal to absorb the real, as with sages, "fastened to a dying animal," the aging body "a sort of battered kettle at the heel." This insight makes possible the summary that opens stanza seven, neatly centered on the nun from stanza one and the mother:

Both nuns and mothers worship images,
But those the candles light are not as those
That animate a mother's reveries,
But keep a marble or a bronze repose.
And yet they too break hearts . . .

In or out of the process of generation, in love with animate or inanimate versions of the ideal, we will have our hearts broken. The Maud Gonnes will break them, our children will break them, so will the centaurs and swans and staring virgins. In a sense, the poem has reached its conclusion. But we are in midstanza and midline, and we have begun to shift from the rhetoric of question to the rhetoric of assertion. As Yeats gathers himself through the remaining three-and-a-half lines of stanza seven to address all the images, we are uncertain about whether he will utter a prayer—a plea for help or for mercy—or a reproach, so mixed are his epithets:

> . . . O Presences
> That passion, piety or affection knows,
> And that all heavenly glory symbolise—
> O self-born mockers of man's enterprise.

The most intriguing phrase here is "self-born." It can mean "giving birth to themselves" and therefore free of the generative process that entraps the mothers and children and philosophers, and it can mean "born of the self," generated by the self's dream of an ideal outside time and mortality. We need to go both ways with the phrase, since the first shows us the apparent difference that makes the mockery possible (it is the difference between Pythagoras and the careless Muses, for example, or the difference between flesh and marble), and the second reminds us, once more, that a person tends to frustrate himself through his own images of perfection, that he or she is really the source of the imagined perfection, the translunar paradise he made when he "made up the whole . . . out of his bitter soul." If he asserts his authority over those images, his authorship, they surely cannot break his heart.

The assertion of authority is what seems to be happening in the famous final stanza. It projects a kind of defiance that insists on a definition of the ideal conditions and seems to imply that the Presences must conform to them:

> Labour is blossoming or dancing where
> The body is not bruised to pleasure soul,

Nor beauty born out of its own despair,
Nor blear-eyed wisdom out of midnight oil.

It is not necessity, the poem seems to claim, that the body must be bruised to pleasure the soul, "Nor beauty born out of its own despair" (note the echo of "self-born," mocking the mockers), nor wisdom out of midnight oil (a remarkable metonymy). The poem has acknowledged the frequency with which process, change, and time take their toll and force the real and ideal apart. But it defies the urge to turn frequency into necessity.

The last half of the last stanza again uses juxtaposition stunningly. Is Yeats in his two questions still addressing "Presences"? He is and is not, since the tree and the dancer belong to a world of change rather than an artifice of eternity or translunar paradise. Moreover, they take on more particularity than the other "Presences," becoming lovely and singular. Yet they are idealized: dancer and dance *are* separable, since the one is not always involved in the other, and the tree may lose its leaves and cannot always be in blossom. But the transformation whereby beauty is turned from its own despair into a "body swayed to music"; and blear-eyed wisdom becomes "a brightening glance"; and labour, blossoming, and dancing are all caught up in glorification of process is responsible for the exhilaration with which the poem closes. We can see why Yeats's poems tend to be about their own struggles to become complete when we have understood that this poem, along with others in *The Tower*, drives toward a vision of wholeness in which art and the artist, changelessness and change, natural and supernatural, time and eternity reveal an interdependency, a common source, that is both paradoxical and convincing. That Yeats should cast it in the form of questions, one clearly rhetorical (a declaration dis-

guised as a question), the other more open, seems wholly
appropriate:

> O chestnut tree, great rooted blossomer,
> Are you the leaf, the blossom or the bole?
> O body swayed to music, O brightening glance,
> How can we know the dancer from the dance?

8. Sophocles in Ireland

If "Among School Children" has its setting in Yeats's daily life as a senator of the new Irish state, "Colonus' Praise," the poem that follows it, swings back, like "Leda" and the Centaur poem, to the apparently remote world of classical mythology and Greek civilization and to the perspective in which we are beyond cultural ties. This "framing" of life by myth reflects the way Yeats in the schoolroom finds himself preoccupied with "Ledaean" beauty and thoughts of Plato, Aristotle, and Pythagoras. It keeps the collection expansive and inclusive even as it acknowledges crucial anchorings in the poet's own life.

In a sense, however, "Colonus' Praise" goes a step further, for it is a translation of an ode in Sophocles' *Oedipus at Colonus*. A second choral ode from this tragedy will turn up as the final section of an upcoming sequence, "A Man Young and Old." Translation is a new feature in the world of *The Tower*. Yeats has given us his versions of other men's philosophies and paintings, but this is his first outright appropriation from another poet. How a Sophoclean choral ode can fit into the highly personal and intricately designed late work of an Anglo-Irish poet is a dramatic issue in itself. Our first reaction might be that Yeats has slipped up in including a translation, letting his pleasure at having brought off a good version of a Greek tragedy get the better of his judgment about what is appropriate for *The Tower*. A closer look, however, convinces us otherwise.

We can begin by asking why Sophocles might attract Yeats's interest and attention. A long-lived artist (ninety years), Sophocles survived a time of great change, from the Athenian victories over the Persians through some fifty years of peace and prosperity and on, from about his sixty-fifth year, to the debilitating Peloponnesian civil war. Throughout these times of change he was able to play a significant role in his society, both as a citizen and as an artist. *Oedipus at Colonus* was written late in his life, and it shows his artistic powers and ability to act as cultural spokesman sustaining themselves with unabated vigor. To the troubled old man, the modernist poet and Irish senator whose dilemmas are dramatized in *The Tower*, Sophocles would be an attractive figure, a model for the artist surviving into old age as a vigorous practitioner of his art and a committed member of his culture.

But another old man is involved, a very different one, whose ultimate fate the play concerns itself with. Oedipus can be seen as a kind of alternative self to Sophocles, just as the blind artists, Raftery and Homer, have been to Yeats. Instead of having a secure part in a flourishing culture, he is alienated from his native Thebes and finds himself, as *Oedipus at Colonus* begins, in a problematic relation to Athens. His age, suffering, and blindness are a curse, but his indomitable spirit gives him a magical significance that will allow him, when Theseus accepts and protects him on behalf of Athens, to bring divine gifts and blessings to that city. He is both less and more than his maker—less secure and stable but more sacred through his associations with nature and with the gods, and finally a greater contributor to the welfare of the community.

The analogy between Sophocles and Oedipus strongly resembles the relation between the Yeats who makes and controls the poems of *The Tower* and the Yeats inside them, who suffers, rages, and is beset, as Oedipus is, by memories and daemonic images. Simply by choosing this playwright and this play, Yeats has set up an interesting model for the artistic strategies and dramatized situations that characterize *The Tower*.

The choral ode, which Yeats has titled "Colonus' Praise," is the first in the play, although it comes when the action is quite far along, just after Theseus' assurances of protection to Oedipus. The guarantee of Athenian hospitality seems to provide the signal for a celebratory account of the harmonious relation between humanity and nature that prevails in the special region to which Oedipus has come. It is a moment when drama turns into lyric, which is what "Two Songs from a Play" was, and what the tension between unfolding drama and exhilarated formal expression through the whole of *The Tower* has been about. In that sense, the ode does not seem jarring, scarcely different from the manner and tone of *The Tower* as we have come to know them, despite the fact that it is a translation from a play over two thousand years old.

On the level of diction and imagery, we soon realize, this poem is thronged with echoes of the poems that have preceded it in the volume.[25] Such details as horses, immortal ladies, and the "wine dark of the wood's intricacies" in the first stanza recall "Nineteen Hundred and Nineteen," the black centaur poem, and the just-concluded "Among School Children." We think of the "fabulous, formless darkness" of "Two Songs from a Play," and the "forest loam" and "dark night" of "Fragments." The ladies suggest Loie Fuller and her dancers, Herodias' daughters, the ladies on unicorns at the end of "Meditations in Time of Civil War," the "lords and ladies of Byzantium," and, of course, the dancer image that has just closed "Among School Children":

> Come praise Colonus' horses and come praise
> The wine dark of the wood's intricacies,
> The nightingale that deafens daylight there,
> If daylight ever visit where,
> Unvisited by tempest or by sun,
> Immortal ladies tread the ground
> Dizzy with harmonious sound,
> Semele's lad a gay companion.

In its rich and dreamy sonorities and pictorially presented mythic landscape, the poem resembles "On a Picture of a Black Centaur by Edmund Dulac" more than the spirited reporting of "Among School Children" or the concentrated violence of "Leda and the Swan." The tonal resemblances thus particularly help recall "the black margin of the wood," the "horse-play," and the "full-flavored wine" of the former poem. Both seem to involve an entranced contemplation of visionary states and meanings. In a sense, we are allowed by "Colonus' Praise" to connect the "Presences" of "Among School Children" to the centaur more firmly than would otherwise have been possible.

In the second stanza we hear about Athene's sacred olive tree:

> And yonder in the gymnasts' garden thrives
> The self-sown, self-begotten shape that gives
> Athenian intellect its mastery,
> Even the grey-leaved olive-tree
> Miracle-bred out of the living stone;

Nor accident of peace nor war
Shall wither that old marvel, for
The great grey-eyed Athene stares thereon.

Recalling the lost artifacts of "Nineteen Hundred and Nine-
teen," among them the "Ancient image made of olive wood,"
we realize that this stanza expresses a misplaced confidence.
At the same time we recognize that "self-sown, self-begotten"
constitutes a useful gloss on "self-born mockers of man's en-
terprise" in "Among School Children." And the word "stares"
summons up a rich chain of associations for us: blind men
and staring virgins, children staring at a sixty-year-old smil-
ing public man, the empty house of the stare, the frustrated
poet pacing the battlements of his tower and staring out
at the landscape. That Sophocles' choral ode can speak so
naturally to issues and contexts of *The Tower* is in itself
entrancing.

The ode's third stanza celebrates not only Athenian toler-
ance and order, but a society that is willing to found its val-
ues on the miraculous and inexplicable, that knows that
mourning and loss are somehow bound up with beauty:

Who comes into this country, and has come
Where golden crocus and narcissus bloom,
Where the Great Mother, mourning for her daughter
And beauty-drunken by the water
Glittering among grey-leaved olive trees
Has plucked a flower and sung her loss;
Who finds abounding Cephisus
Has found the loveliest spectacle there is.

The issue that *The Tower* began with—"That is no country for
old men"—is here addressed by reiterating that life and death,
beauty and loss, are part of the same whole. Whether Athens
and Colonus will be a country for an old man like Oedipus is

precisely the issue. The ode is a moment of celebration but not of dramatic resolution, since Oedipus will be haunted by visitors from Thebes—Creon and Polyneices—in the remaining part of *Oedipus at Colonus*, much as the old man who has found a measure of uneasy social acceptance, "a comfortable kind of old scarecrow," is haunted by phantoms of memory and obsession in "Among School Children."

The fact that the ode does not mark the moment when Oedipus' problems are solved by his accommodation with Athens is reflected in a larger perspective by our knowledge that what is celebrated is beautiful indeed but not, as the Chorus hopes (and as Sophocles hoped), enduring. Colonus is right to have a "pious mind" and remember its gifts from Athene, mastery of intellect, and Poseidon, bit and oar (horse taming and navigation), but man is in love and loves what vanishes, and even Athens is no exception. The play's deeper significance is expressed by the ravaged and doomed figure of Oedipus himself, and in the context of *The Tower*, where the choral ode recedes into the mythic distance of other "ingenious lovely things" that have vanished, it has meanings it could not have in its original setting or at the time of its original performance:

> Because this country has a pious mind
> And so remembers that when all mankind
> But trod the road, or paddled by the shore,
> Poseidon gave it bit and oar,
> Every Colonus lad or lass discourses
> Of that oar and of that bit;
> Summer and winter, day and night,
> Of horses and horses of the sea, white horses.

We are meant to admire and assent to this, even as we cannot ignore meanings of bit and oar—"violence of horses," "the mackerel-crowded seas"—that qualify the sense of security and celebration. The ways in which "Colonus' Praise" takes its place in the dialogues and dialectics of *The Tower* are finally most impressive.

Oedipus seems also to open up the topics of love and sexuality, for the next three poems by the order I am following —"The Fool by the Roadside," "Owen Aherne and His Dancers," and the sequence "A Man Young and Old"—all have those themes, and the sequence itself ends with a second choral ode from *Oedipus at Colonus*, to reinforce the relationship. These three poems have their differences, but they share a tendency to examine human passions in a kind of abstract theater, where properties and setting are of the simplest kind.[26]

"The Fool by the Roadside" exists in a longer version, "The Hero, the Girl, and the Fool," which has been in the standard *Collected Poems* for some years now but has recently been cast out on the grounds that Yeats preferred the short version.[27] The stylized characters in both versions are too generalized to engage us very fully. The longer version is a sort of miniature play in two acts. The first demonstrates love's self-divisions while the second affirms the unlikeliness of perfect love in this world. The Hero and Girl speak to each other; the Fool sings or speaks to himself, functioning as a kind of chorus.

In the longer version, the Girl rages "at my own image in the glass" because she fears that it, rather than her true self, has captured the Hero's love; the Hero, it turns out, has entertained similar doubts about her idealization of his strength. The impasse does not stress suffering, however, as their colloquy modulates to a witty exchange.

The Fool's half, now on its own as a lyric, runs as follows:

THE FOOL BY THE ROADSIDE

When my days that have
From cradle run to grave
From grave to cradle run instead;

When thoughts that a fool
Has wound upon a spool
Are but loose thread, are but loose thread;

When cradle and spool are past
And I mere shade at last
Coagulate of stuff
Transparent like the wind,
I think that I may find
A faithful love, a faithful love.

In the older version this was a choric comment on the lovers. By itself it offers a pessimistic conclusion cast in a lyric form that suggests acceptance and joy, a quality that attracted Yeats to the Sophoclean tragic odes and that reflects a tension between form and content characteristic of *The Tower* as a whole but often easier to identify in short poems like "Fragments," "The Wheel," and this one. It is the tension produced by offering images, situations, and insights that are in themselves gloomy or frightening or disorienting in lyric forms that suggest delight and celebration. Associations with the theater and the tension between actor's art and character's fate were added in "Two Songs from a Play" and repeated in the Sophoclean choral ode. The Fool by the roadside is a fool in the world's terms both because he is an outcast, with the alienated wisdom of a beggar or vagrant, and because he does not seem to know enough to be upset by the absence of faithful love in this life. In theatrical terms, of course, he is a wise fool, in the Shakespearean mode, one who understands what Yeats would later come to describe as "tragic joy."

The Shakespearean fool who knows tragic joy is of course the one in *King Lear*, and there is something Lear-like about the characters and situation of the next poem, "Owen Aherne and his Dancers." It has an autobiographical base in the tumultuous series of events (proposal to Iseult Gonne, who was

17, refusal; proposal to George Hyde-Lees, acceptance) that led to Yeats's marriage, but that is really of no great interest in its present context, where it stands as an earlier poem (1917) brought into the context of youth and age and their incessant struggle in *The Tower*.

Aherne tells us that "when love had come unsought / Upon the Norman upland or in that poplar shade" his heart had no burden but itself to bear and yet, incapable, had gone mad. The love dialogue of the previous lyric continues; the image of madness in a natural setting is what seems to echo *Lear*, with the *Oedipus at Colonus* beyond it. Raging old men are welcome to populate *The Tower*, as we know, whether they come from life or literature. Through the rest of the first section Aherne speaks with wonder of his normal sanity and health as against the sudden and unforeseen madness of his heart.

In the second section, the heart has its chance to respond. It derides the idea that the old man of fifty could even think of mating with one "that was so wildly bred." Aherne, now married, defends his new wife against the implicit charge of being a "cage bird," and worries about how she would respond to knowing that his thoughts "are far away." The heart encourages candor:

'Speak all your mind,' my Heart sang out, 'speak all your mind;
    who cares,
Now that your tongue cannot persuade the child till she mistake
Her childish gratitude for love and match your fifty years.
O let her choose a young man now and all for his wild sake.'

As thinly disguised autobiography, this is of rather limited interest. As part of the dramatization of old age and its frustrations and reconciliations, it is effectively placed in the great sequence of *The Tower*. The reader may well wonder who the dancers are and how they fit into a poem that never mentions them beyond the title. In the autobiographical reading, we can remind ourselves that Iseult Gonne was a dancer, but that still does not account for the plural. In the context of *The Tower*, however, we have an image of life itself as a dance. "All men are dancers," as we learned from meditating on Loie Fuller, and dancer and dance have been the complex answer to the problems of time and aging in "Among School Children." Aherne's dancers are the women he loves but they are also the parts of himself—heart, tongue, mind—liberated to movements and harmonies of their own, to a designed opposition that looks at first like conflict but resolves itself into the kind of patterned speech and response of theater and the turn and counterturn of dance, the exchange of line for line and stanza for stanza in the lyric, the dance from poem to poem in *The Tower*.

9. The Death of the Hare

While there are a number of lengthy poems in *The Tower*, some in numbered sections, there are two that properly deserve the term "sequence," meaning a number of individual lyrics with their own titles, grouped under a comprehensive title. "Meditations in Time of Civil War," the first, is placed in a comparable relation to the second, "A Man Young and Old," the one coming third from the beginning, the other third from the end, in the final version. Their common form and analogous placement invite comparison, and their differences help us see how some of the tones and attitudes of *The Tower* have shifted. Especially following "Among School Children" the volume has adopted a more lyrical manner, that is to say, both more songlike and more celebratory. Old age is still a problem, but the sense of being reconciled to it, even at times delighted with it, permeates "A Man Young and Old." History is still a gigantic pageant of devastating change, but its depredations scarcely affect the lifespan adumbrated in this second sequence, which could belong to a number of historical periods and still hold its validity. And the cultural problems that beset the aging Yeats when he addressed himself to the question of what his poetry should be like have been temporarily set aside. The poet who has been able to recreate myth so confidently in "Leda and the Swan," address the Centaur as an equal, defy the heart-breaking Presences that haunt the classroom and the memory in "Among School Children," and invoke the ecstatic note of late Sophoclean tragedy here turns to stylized treatments of a world in which love cannot sustain itself and human beings have little to expect but sorrow and decay—treatments that belie, in their exquisite gaiety, their own bitter meanings.

"Meditations" emphasized the poet's solitude and uncertainty, along with insoluble problems of inheritance and the continuity of civilized achievement. It took its place perfectly between "The Tower" and "Nineteen Hundred and Nineteen." "A Man Young and Old," which universalizes the human condition with a few simple properties, type characters, and a peasant persona, says nothing to contradict the insights of the earlier sequence, but it implies, being unweighted by them, that they can be set aside. Its context, too, makes it the more meaningful.

Given what has just been said, I think it important to deemphasize Unterecker's notion that "A Man Young and Old," like "Owen Aherne and His Dancers," is autobiographical. To search these poems for the poet's experiences and relationships is to turn away from both their abstractness and their figurative thrust. Unterecker is much more helpful when he calls attention to the way "A Man Young and Old" is "held together by a set of interrelated images."[28] The reader's challenge, as with the larger model, *The Tower*, is to help the poems cohere, to find their interrelationships. Again, background knowledge may help or hinder. If we know that the first four pieces were originally published under the title "Four Songs from the Young Countryman," we may make too sharp a distinction between those four and the next seven. As soon as Yeats gave the whole group the overall title "A Man Young and Old," suggesting an entire lifespan, he blurred the distinction between whether a young or old man is speaking at any given point. The result was to set up a youth-age dialectic that is present at every point. The sequence suggests a progression, to be sure, but it also has constants, mixing the perspectives of youth and age as it goes. A man may be young or old, runs the implicit claim, and he may be both when in age he relives or recalls his own youth.

Here, for example, is the first of the group:

I. *First Love*

Though nurtured like the sailing moon
In beauty's murderous brood,
She walked awhile and blushed awhile
And on my pathway stood
Until I thought her body bore
A heart of flesh and blood.

But since I laid a hand thereon
And found a heart of stone
I have attempted many things
And not a thing is done,
For every hand is lunatic
That travels on the moon.

She smiled and that transfigured me
And left me but a lout,
Maundering here, and maundering there,
Emptier of thought
Than the heavenly circuit of its stars
When the moon sails out.

When this is part of a group called "Four Songs from a Young Countryman," any difference in perspective between the experience of first love and the lyric's detached commentary on

that experience is apt to be attributed to the difference be-
tween the lover speaking and the poet who has shaped the
lyric. When it joins a sequence called "A Man Young and
Old," the distinction between character and artist is harder
to discern. The perspective on first love now becomes the per-
spective of age as well as art, and the implicit joining of art
and old age constitutes a pervasive resolution to the problem
of the aging poet that *The Tower* has been so preoccupied
with. Each takes strength from the other. To be an artist is to
gain a superior vantage point on the tumultuous world. To be
old is to experience the same privilege. Pain becomes song.
The speaker's transfiguration to a "lout" in this poem reminds
us of the fool by the roadside and the implicit wisdom of folly
when it has gone to its own extreme or has been stylized for
dramatic purposes.

We also note that an object may be beautiful or murderous,
depending on circumstances. The stone heart and the sailing
moon are really the same object. Touching the one has left
the speaker "lunatic" because it has also meant touching the
other, but his transfiguration eventually has cosmic mean-
ings too, even if he is only the night sky made empty of stars
through the dominance of moonlight. The moon image sets
up an effective transition to the second poem:

II. *Human Dignity*

Like the moon her kindness is,
If kindness I may call
What has no comprehension in't,
But is the same for all
As though my sorrow were a scene
Upon a painted wall.

So like a bit of stone I lie
Under a broken tree.
I could recover if I shrieked

My heart's agony
To passing bird, but I am dumb
From human dignity.

Our delight in this is manifold. We encounter the self-pity of
youthful love being teased by the manner of its treatment. To
the reader of *The Tower* there is the additional interest of
seeing the poem assembled from scraps of earlier ones. The
broken tree was part of the view from the Tower, which also
overlooked an acre of stony ground and, now and again, a
moonlit scene. Passing birds and heart's agony are equally fa-
miliar, and the issue of human dignity has been before us
in more serious terms than that of a speechless lover lying
under a tree.

I do not mean to imply that Yeats has no reaction but
mockery to offer the young lover, merely that he uses, as so
often, a double perspective achieved by disparities of form
and content and by the implied dialectics of life and art,
youth and age. In the landscape the volume opened with, the
old man felt he had no true place; it was all "the young / In
one another's arms." The young man might well complain
that this austere world of stone, moon, shrieking birds, and
broken trees is no country for young men. And yet his experi-
ence is the focus of the sequence.

As if to show us that such matters could be treated even
more succinctly, the third poem relates the experiences of
first love and rejection in the form of a fable:

III. *The Mermaid*

A mermaid found a swimming lad,
Picked him for her own,
Pressed her body to his body,
Laughed; and plunging down
Forgot in cruel happiness
That even lovers drown.[29]

Is this more of the young man's self-pity, lightly disguised, or is it a demonstration of the ability to fable, to imagine successfully, the special gift of old age? The reader will recognize how much the latter question informs *The Tower* as a whole.

The fourth poem is the most difficult in the sequence, at least for any definitive interpretation. The biographical reading of it identifies the hare as Iseult Gonne and locates the speaker's dilemma in having to divide his attention between two women.[30] But this stresses both symbolism and biography in a way that seems inappropriate to *The Tower*.

IV. *The Death of the Hare*

I have pointed out the yelling pack,
The hare leap to the wood,
And when I pass a compliment
Rejoice as lover should
At the drooping of an eye,
At the mantling of the blood.

Then suddenly my heart is wrung
By her distracted air
And I remember wildness lost
And after, swept from there,
Am set down standing in the wood
At the death of the hare.

The comparison of wild hunt and decorous lovers is startling. We think of the dialectic between caged and wild as attributes of lovers in "Owen Aherne and His Dancers" and, further back, the "wild infancy" of Christ, the heart driven wild by memories of love in "Among School Children," the "wild nest" of the mother bird in "The Tower." The lover who speaks here seems to think he has put the wildness of love behind him until association suddenly sweeps him to a wild scene, the climax of the hunt and the death of the hare, the moment when wildness is destroyed. Is the death of the hare, the destruction of the wild thing, the death of love as well? The mermaid's destructiveness was one demonstration of love's murderous innocence. Is this another?

There is, at any rate, no need to bring Iseult Gonne or Mrs. Yeats into it, any more than we would bring them into "Leda and the Swan." We are on a very generalized level, even more so than with characters like Red Hanrahan and Lady Kyteler. And "wildness lost" must mean both the destructiveness of the hunt, love's unthinking pursuit, and the agony of having love only as a memory. Asked once to interpret this lyric, Yeats refused, adding: "If an author interprets a poem of his own he limits its suggestibility. You can say that the lover may, while loving, feel sympathy with his beloved's dread of captivity. I don't know how else to put it."[31] It is a useful way to put it because it sends us back to the careful diction: "drooping" and "mantling" refer to a world of courtship and coquetry—"mantling" is an old word for blushing—but they also belong to the language of falconry, the systematic taming of a wild creature—"mantling" is a form of exercise used for captive birds, who may of course "droop" in captivity. We have switched from the theme of the woman's innocent destructiveness in the opening lyrics to the fact that something is always lost when a man begins to assert command, even a lover's tender mastery, over a woman. Love continues to be partly a power struggle, but male self-pity has been exchanged for the larger recognition (in a male, at any rate) of male predation.

The next poem, "The Empty Cup," uses fable or parable again. A man dying of thirst is afraid to drink from the cup he finds because he imagines, "moon accursed," that he has already drunk too much. Love has confused him into rejecting his own youth and, we conjecture, proffered sexual re-

lease. The aged narrator, more knowledgeable, has the ill for-
tune to find the cup empty:

> October last I found it too
> But found it dry as bone,
> And for that reason am I crazed
> And my sleep is gone.

There seems to be no way out of love's dilemmas. If we pursue
love we may be crazed and drowned, and if we succeed in
finding it we may destroy an innocent wildness. But if we
shun it, we will only live to regret the empty cup of old age.
The sequence has reached a kind of crisis point. It will now
turn from the agonies of love in youth to some sense of the
compensations of old age.

Section 6, "His Memories," shows how memories—and it
matters little whether they're accurate or embroidered by the
passage of time—can sustain an old scarecrow who is a fig-
ure of fun and a grotesque image:

> My arms are like the twisted thorn
> And yet there beauty lay;
> The first of all the tribe lay there
> And did such pleasure take—
> She who had brought great Hector down
> And put all Troy to wreck—
> That she cried into this ear
> Strike me if I shriek.[32]

We have gone from someone who found the sexual grail only
when it was empty to someone who has a secret cup to drink
from as often as he likes. The Ledaean beauty he has enjoyed
has destroyed neither him nor the woman he gave pleasure
to, so that the memories seem to survive undiminished in
value and meaning.

This old man's world, however, if it is lit by the secret compensations of memory, is a strange and unsettling place. It would not be like Yeats to portray it as unequivocally valuable, although he keeps the note of crack-pated gaiety right through to the end. In the seventh section definite characters appear, and the compensations of age contain a rather harsh mixture of the vindictive:

> Laughter not time destroyed my voice
> And put that crack in it,
> And when the moon's pot-bellied
> I get a laughing fit,
> For that old Madge comes down the lane
> A stone upon her breast,
> And a cloak wrapped about the stone,
> And she can get no rest
> With singing hush and hush-a-bye;
> She that has been wild
> And barren as a breaking wave
> Thinks that the stone's a child.

This is effective both for the way it weaves together earlier details—stone, moon, wildness, and water—and for the way it mixes pleasure at the senility of the woman figure, who had earlier caused the man's suffering through her indifference and beauty, with an implied pathos that envelops them both. The grotesque emphasis continues:

> And Peter that had great affairs
> And was a pushing man
> Shrieks, 'I am King of the Peacocks,'
> And perches on a stone;
> And then I laugh till tears run down
> And the heart thumps at my side,
> Remembering that her shriek was love
> And that he shrieks from pride.

Age is a kind of leveler, but the running tears and thumping heart keep us in touch with other possibilities than the cackling glee of the speaker; there is still something of the young man in the old man, and he can remember the love-shriek and distinguish it from the shriek of self-love. The peacock is new to the sequence, but not to the reader of *The Tower*.

The next two sections, "Summer and Spring," and "The Secrets of the Old," keep the youth-age dialectic alive while continuing the gradual modulation toward acceptance and even celebration of old age. "Summer and Spring" is especially interesting for its reprise of the moment of youthful oneness depicted in the second section of "Among School Children":

> We sat under an old thorn-tree
> And talked away the night,
> Told all that had been said or done
> Since first we saw the light,
> And when we talked of growing up
> Knew that we'd halved a soul
> And fell the one in t'other's arms
> That we might make it whole.

Again, the recollection is sustaining and the perspective half-humorous. The ninth lyric, "The Secrets of the Old," argues that the speaker can now know women's secrets, things "I dared not think / When my blood was strong": his knowledge is androgynous and it embraces the experience of all social classes, "Stories of the bed of straw / Or the bed of down." Once more, age's perspective is much the same as art's.

In section 10, "His Wildness," the original ending of the poem, Yeats manages again a marvelous recycling of the poem's images and another reversal of emotional possibility:

> O bid me mount and sail up there
> Amid the cloudy wrack,

For Peg and Meg and Paris' love
That had so straight a back,
Are gone away, and some that stay,
Have changed their silk for sack.

This is that recognition embodied in "The Wheel" that "what disturbs our blood / Is but its longing for the tomb." The speaker's willingness to say good-bye to the world may not be, as in "Nineteen Hundred and Nineteen," "a rage to end all things"; it is quieter and more exultant. He is now ready to be serene and distant as the moon, qualities of the lovely woman who was his tormentor at the outset of the sequence. But distance, once perceived as indifference, turns out to contain an extraordinary measure of sympathy, a purging of the harsh laughter expressed in section 11:

Were I but there and none to hear
I'd have a peacock cry,
For that is natural to a man
That lives in memory,
Being all alone I'd nurse a stone
And sing it lullaby.

The torment of identity laid by, he can be Madge or Peter with ease. The moon that "pitches common things about" and that lit the phantoms of hatred and the heart's fullness in the last section of "Meditations in Time of Civil War" does not free him completely from earth—he will still cry like a peacock and nurse a stone—but it resolves the dilemmas of youth and age that the poem has placed before us. The resolution may recall "Sailing to Byzantium," but its terms are wholly those of this rusticated lyric sequence.

After first including it separately in *The Tower* (after "The Three Monuments" and before "The Gift of Harun Al-Rashid"), Yeats decided to incorporate another choral ode from *Oedipus at Colonus* as the last section of "A Man Young and Old." Again, this decision sounds an unlikely one that reveals, on closer scrutiny, Yeats's confident sense at this period of what he could and could not juxtapose.

Using the ode to close the sequence accomplishes several things. It recapitulates the sequence in terms of a different mode of speaking and thinking. The lines grow long; the folksong or "peasant" manner changes to a more measured classical style; and the voice, a choric voice, becomes impersonal. The whole effect is of an overview and summary that bring "human dignity" back to the questions of old age:

> Endure what life God gives and ask no longer span;
> Cease to remember the delights of youth, travel-wearied aged man;
> Delight becomes death-longing if all longing else be vain.

This is something like the emotional pitch on which the sequence ended in section 10, translated into the late Sophoclean manner. The ode goes on to repeat this insight three times, in various forms, while we divide our attention between its relevance to Sophocles' tragedy on the one hand and its relevance to this sequence and to *The Tower* on the other:

> Even from that delight memory treasures so,
> Death, despair, division of families, all entanglements of mankind grow,
> As that old wandering beggar and these God-hated children know.
>
> In the long echoing street the laughing dancers throng,
> The bride is carried to the bridegroom's chamber through torchlight and tumultuous song;
> I celebrate the silent kiss that ends short life or long.

In life, delight and despair are inseparable, and the dancers in the long street give us a resonant image that carries that inseparability vividly because it has so many echoes of other poems in *The Tower*.

Yeats brings his rather free translation to a close with some of the most famous literary sentiments ever expressed:

> Never to have lived is best, ancient writers say;
> Never to have drawn the breath of life, never to have looked into
>   the eye of day;
> The second best's a gay goodnight and quickly turn away.

The ode carries the tendencies of both the sequence and the volume to a decisive conclusion, detaching Yeats at the same time, since he is present neither as character nor author, merely as translator. The inclusion of this poem in the sequence is like the inclusion of "Colonus' Praise" in the volume, and serves in turn to remind us how much the two long sequences—"Meditations in Time of Civil War" and "A Man Young and Old"—reflect in their designs and juxtapositions the methods of *The Tower* itself.

The theme of old age, which opened *The Tower* and recurred throughout, reaches a culmination in "A Man Young and Old." The sequence shows us that a man may be *both* young and old. That can be problematic—bodily decrepitude housing an active imagination, vindictiveness, self-love and self-pity, torment by memories of loss and failure. But it can also be splendid—wisdom, mastery of memory and experience, the perspective of an artist, soul clapping its hands and singing "for every tatter in its mortal dress." Whatever the result, a man cannot be both young and old until he is old. He needs age before he can even hope to judge the question of whether youth or age is preferable. *The Tower* moves to equivocal affirmations of old age through recognition of its inevitability and its potential to retain and refine as well as to lose. That is the lesson of such various models as *Oedipus at Colonus*, "Sailing to Byzantium," and "Among School Children."

10. Muscatel in Oxford

"A Man Young and Old" is followed by a short poem with a political emphasis, "The Three Monuments":

They hold their public meetings where
Our most renowned patriots stand,
One among the birds of the air,
A stumpier one on either hand;
And all the popular statesmen say
That purity built up the state
And after kept it from decay;
Admonish us to cling to that
And let all base ambition be,
For intellect would make us proud
And pride bring in impurity:
The three old rascals laugh aloud.

The poem is topical (arising from the debate in the Irish Senate on a divorce bill in which Yeats had spoken against the hypocrisy of Irish political morality) and sardonic: it earns

its place in *The Tower* by giving us yet another version of the
special perspectives of old age. The statues of Lord Nelson,
Thomas Parnell, and Daniel O'Connell, "old rascals" all,
join the throng of scarecrows, beggars, philosophers, and rag-
ing oldsters that populate *The Tower*. At the center of this
group is the figure of the poet, sedentary and often baffled,
but touched by visions and magical powers of the kind that
cluster around Oedipus. The disillusion and despair of "Nine-
teen Hundred and Nineteen" do not afflict him. That statues
should come to life seems appropriate to the sense of wonder
and accomplishment fostered by *The Tower*; that they should
do so in order to laugh out loud at human folly is equally fit-
ting, linking them with the sixty-year-old smiling public
man who can be wry about bodily decrepitude even as he
celebrates the powers of imagination.

At this point in the first edition of *The Tower* stands a poem
of some two hundred lines, "The Gift of Harun Al-Rashid."
Yeats experimented with that placement and with the alter-
native, familiar to most readers, of putting it last in the "Nar-
rative and Dramatic" section of the *Collected Poems*. Since
the latter option has led to its obscurity and neglect, and
since it clearly belongs, in its themes and preoccupations, to
the period in which the poems in the volume were written, I
think it deserves at least a brief consideration in its original
place. Being narrative in manner—it purports to be a letter
to a friend by an aging philosopher-poet who tells the story
of his marriage late in life—it lacks the intensity and com-
pression of most of the poems in *The Tower*. But the variety of
the volume—as expressed by the presence of long and short
pieces, sequences, songs, translations, prayers, and medita-
tions—would surely seem to accommodate a narrative that
invokes the exotic cultures (one thinks of Byzantium and
Babylon) treated in shorter lyrics. It may be true that from
the biographical point of view it is "almost painfully alle-

gorical" in its treatment of Yeats's own marriage, but to the attentive reader of *The Tower* it offers a number of other perspectives as well.[33]

The political cast of "The Three Monuments" is briefly echoed in a completely different setting, as Kusta ben Luka, the poet-mage, relates that his young bride was a gift from the powerful and mysterious ruler whose name gives the poem its title. Harun Al-Rashid, like Alexander the Great, has destroyed a friend for no apparent reason; he is a figure of mysterious tyranny, an embodiment of fate, perhaps, but also, to Kusta ben Luka, a man who may be mellowing:

> . . . Enough for me
> That in the early summer of the year
> The mightiest of the princes of the world
> Came to the least considered of his courtiers;
> Sat down upon the fountain's marble edge
> One hand amid the goldfish in the pool;
> And thereupon a colloquy took place
> That I commend to all the chroniclers
> To show how violent great hearts can lose
> Their bitterness and find the honeycomb.

The diction and the preoccupations—fountains, violent great hearts, bitterness, honeycomb—are very reminiscent of "Meditations in Time of Civil War." The colloquy that follows is a kind of dialogue of self and soul, contrasting the values of the worldly and sensual ruler and the old scholar bent on eternal truths and mysteries. Harun Al-Rashid offers a bride who shares the fascination with "those old crabbed mysteries" that preoccupy Kusta ben Luka. After their marriage she begins to speak at night, in her sleep, with the voice of "some great Djinn" (note his vagueness about the source), articulating the mysteries for which he has searched all his life:

Self-born, high-born, and solitary truths,
Those terrible implacable straight lines
Drawn through the wandering vegetative dream,
Even those truths that when my bones are dust
Must drive the Arabian host.

The twist that the story now takes is that Kusta ben Luka's fear grows to be not that he will lose his contact with divine mysteries but that he will lose her love:

What if she lose her ignorance and so
Dream that I love her only for the voice,
That every gift and every word of praise
Is but a payment for that midnight voice
That is to age what milk is to a child?

The point is that she is not simply a conduit for truths and mysteries, but a source as well:

      . . . The voice has drawn
A quality of wisdom from her love's
Particular quality. The signs and shapes;
All those abstractions that you fancied were
From the great Treatise of Parmenides;
All, all those gyres and cubes and midnight things
Are but a new expression of her body
Drunk with the bitter sweetness of her youth.

This is an insight that Harun Al-Rashid had foreseen when he spoke of a poet's thought "That springs from body and in body falls" like the fountain they sat by, "Like this pure jet, now lost amid blue sky, / Now bathing lily leaf and fish's scale." Kusta's friend has been instructed to hide the letter for posterity in the Treatise of Parmenides, but the message it will pass down is that opposites are interdependent, and that

their marriage, as reflected in the one described in the poem—
a marriage of youth and age, wisdom and beauty, male and
female—is a truer thing than "gyres and cubes and midnight
things."

Kusta ben Luka's dilemma is a mirror to the paradoxical
world of *The Tower*. He has finally discovered "Self-born,
high-born and solitary truths," but that discovery, instead of
freeing him from this life and its concerns, has plunged him
deeper into illusory, temporal existence. Truth's vehicle—a
combination of youth, beauty and womanhood—is not
something he can ignore, any more than one can separate
dancer from dance. Like the aging poet of "Meditations" and
"Among School Children," he must accept process, time, illu-
sion, and mortality as indispensable to any knowledge of
what lies beyond them. Moreover, the dialectic is inces-
sant; both the "straight lines" and the "wandering vegetative
dream" are necessary to art and knowledge. The aching
heart produces the changeless work of art, but the art reflects
the ache and depends upon it for its meaning, and time will
destroy "ingenious, lovely things" that "seemed sheer mir-
acle" and give rise to a need for more. The real truth or secret
that Kusta has been graced with is the paradox of learning
ultimate mysteries from a contradictory source:

> All, all those gyres and cubes and midnight things
> Are but a new expression of her body
> Drunk with the bitter sweetness of her youth.
> And now my utmost mystery is out.

The case for including this poem in *The Tower*, then and now,
lies in its essential relevance to that book's vision of art and
experience.

While "Gift" somewhat resembles "Sailing to Byzantium"
in its furnishings, it differs considerably in its emphatic re-

turn to the world that at first seemed "no country for old men." In terms of Yeats's life, the poem is no doubt a celebration of his marriage and the peculiar combination of occult discoveries and sensual reawakening it brought. In terms of *The Tower*, it is one more example of Daedalus turning and flying back into the maze he seemed to escape from. "The Gift of Harun Al-Rashid" reads somewhat like a period piece, so that it is a stylistic and formal falling back for the poet, less ostentatiously "modern," more unabashedly "romantic":

> A woman's beauty is a storm-tossed banner;
> Under it wisdom stands, and I alone—
> Of all Arabia's lovers I alone—
> Nor dazzled by the embroidery, nor lost
> In the confusion of its night-dark folds,
> Can hear the armed man speak.

The personification of Wisdom as an armed man echoes the mysterious ruler and gift-giver Harun Al-Rashid, and the imagery recalls the war banners hanging in the palace at the outset of the poem.

The passage also emphasizes the necessary conjunction of violence and wisdom, the role of struggle and dialectic. Even a tranquil old man cannot, it turns out, "be content with argument and deal / In abstract things," living simply among "daemonic images" and "phantoms." Poetry's grounding in the physical world, and the imagination's necessary interaction with the life of the body, are here given a plangent synthesis, but the philosophical discovery belies the tone. Struggle is the other face of tranquillity. This poem also has a comic twist, given its wry portrait of an aging wise man unwilling to admit his sensuality as the source of his wisdom except through a secret letter to posterity, tucked away in a Treatise of Parmenides!

The transition to the final poem of *The Tower*, "All Souls' Night," is very effective when "The Gift of Harun Al-Rashid" is in its original place. The subjects of the occult and of hard-won but paradoxical wisdom are already in mind. The mask of Kusta ben Luka comes off, and we find Yeats in Oxford, eight years before the publication of *The Tower*, thinking of three friends who shared his passionate interest in occult knowledge and who might, therefore, be tempted to visit him from the realm of death.

The poem's subtitle tells us that it is also the epilogue to *A Vision*. Even to a reader unfamiliar with that work, the notation suggests a poem that summarizes the poet's life and thought. As the concluding lyric of the volume under consideration, "All Souls' Night" provides in form, style, and content a sense of closure and resolution that is triumphant and harmonious while continuing to do justice to the complexities of experience that *The Tower* has set before us.

The occasion, as Ellmann has noted, is ritualistic, another summoning of the dead on the night that is traditionally theirs.[34] The means suggest traditional ceremony—at midnight the poet places two glasses of wine on a table, one for himself and one for a ghost or ghosts who need only "the wine-breath" to please their palates. To this ceremony the poet adds variations that are peculiarly Yeatsian; if the ghosts arrive it is much more through the efforts of the poet and his imagination than through traditional magic. The ceremony acts more to furnish his poem and prepare his imagination than actually to contact the supernatural.

The setting, Oxford, is interesting too. It is of course where Yeats and his wife were living when he wrote the poem, their alternative quarters to the tower at Ballylee at that time, but there is an attractive and mischievous effect to setting what would seem to be a "spooky" poem in the great and ancient seat of learning and orthodoxy, within earshot of "the great

Christ Church Bell," booming the strokes of midnight. Yeats may seem donnish and sedentary to us, more at peace than the restless and brooding figure who paced the battlement of the tower, or he may seem like an undergraduate, playing at rituals and sampling wine. Youth and age again, or "Among School Children" at a somewhat more advanced educational level. The poem could have been set in the isolated and equivocal landscape of Thoor Ballylee. By using a scholarly and distinguished setting, Yeats suggests that there is no serious conflict between his spiritualist preoccupations and the more familiar pursuits of a great university. This is the first of a series of resolved antinomies around which the poem is constructed. Oxford is also an interesting setting given Yeats's multiple cultural allegiances; he looks toward Ireland and toward Europe from a quintessentially English setting.

The sense of harmony is much enhanced by the form of the poem. Ten stanzas of ten lines each divide readily into five pairs: the first pair is introductory, the next three pairs are devoted to three potential otherworldly visitors, and the final pair moves to summary and resolution. The pairs tend to alternate the worldly with the otherworldly, and the stanzas themselves more often than not divide at the fifth and sixth lines, changing tone, qualifying statements, or shifting subject. All this symmetry, supported by rhetoric that calls attention to it ("Horton's the first I call . . . On Florence Emery I call the next . . . And I call up MacGregor from the grave"), supports the impression of poetic command and genuine pleasure in a subject that has potential for disorder and terror.[35] The relation of phantoms to reality has never been an easy one in *The Tower*, and the visitations of memory have sometimes been involuntary and unwelcome. In keeping with the progression toward an acceptance of old age, even a celebration of its special rewards, this poem accommodates past and present, natural and supernatural, along with a sense of enjoyment, even merriment, at the prospect of meeting ghosts.

It might even be argued that the poem is weakened by an absence of the kind of conflict that led the speaker of "Sailing to Byzantium" to his extraordinary quest, or the frustration and helplessness out of which celebratory insights like those in "The Tower," "Among School Children," and "A Man Young and Old" were born. That is somewhat like criticizing *The Tempest* because it is not *Hamlet*. If "All Souls' Night" is less dramatic than the major poems of the collection, it has compensations, in its multiplicity of suggestions and possibilities, that should satisfy the most demanding readers.

I find in "All Souls' Night" a faint but unmistakable note of comedy, a note in keeping both with the pleasure and harmony expressed in the poem and with the edge of self-mockery and wry amusement that has been present throughout *The Tower*. In this case, there is some fun at the expense of both speaker and situation. "Yeats" sits expectantly before two bubbling glasses of muscatel (does muscatel bubble?) as the clocks toll midnight. Nothing that happens to the wine will tell him whether he has had a ghostly visitor because only the wine-breath, "The fume of muscatel," will be drunk, with no perceptible change in the wine. He can have a dozen visitors, or none. Next we begin to realize from his thoughts that there is no particular reason that any of the people in question would care to visit him. The effect recalls the crowd of phantoms "impatient to be gone" in "The Tower." Horton was always intent on the other world, anxious to rejoin his lost love; his obsession is a little less grandiose, though no less thoroughgoing, by the time Yeats has found a mundane comparison for the "one sole image" his mind's eye is trained upon:

And that a slight companionable ghost,
Wild with divinity,
Had so lit up the whole
Immense miraculous house
The Bible promised us,
It seemed a gold-fish swimming in a bowl.

The Yeats family had goldfish at Oxford, apparently. To me, the image seems to undercut Horton's faith and quest, affectionately rather than contemptuously.

Florence Emery has also turned away from the world and sought a kind of hermetic existence, enacting a pattern familiar from "Among School Children." Her investigations of the occult have taught her that the soul's journey ends when it can "plunge into the sun" and leave this world behind:

And there, free and yet fast
Being both Chance and Choice,
Forget its broken toys
And sink into its own delight at last.

Florence Emery may have to undergo more incarnations, but the image scarcely suggests that her ghost will be hanging around Oxford on the chance of picking up some muscatel fumes. At the same time it defines once again the differences between time and eternity that have preoccupied us so often throughout *The Tower*.

MacGregor (S. L. MacGregor Mathers) turns out to have quarreled with Yeats and become increasingly eccentric:

He had much industry at setting out,
Much boisterous courage, before loneliness
Had driven him crazed;
For meditations upon unknown thought

Make human intercourse grow less and less;
They are neither paid nor praised.
But he'd object to the host,
The glass because my glass;
A ghost-lover he was
And may have grown more arrogant being a ghost.

Though Yeats thinks of him fondly and forgivingly, there is not much indication that this is likely to be reciprocated, and that this particular All Souls' Night will see a reunion of the youthful friends.

But the whole enterprise has been doubtful from the outset. The speaker has said that he needs "some mind that . . . can stay / Wound in mind's pondering," and we are not quite sure whether he means his own or that of a ghostly visitor, though the former seems more likely, given the last stanza. The image of being wound in mind's pondering "as mummies in the mummy-cloth are wound" is in itself equivocal; the wrapping suggests muffling, the kind of labyrinth that Yeats has said, in "Nineteen Hundred and Nineteen," we make for ourselves before we know enough to bid the world good-bye. The image recurs at the end, but with "pondering" changed to a less impressive activity:

I need no other thing
Wound in mind's wandering,
As mummies in the mummy-cloth are wound.

The dead whom the speaker imagines as visiting have presumably been unwound, freed of the wrappings of life ("When thoughts that a fool / Has wound upon a spool / Are but loose thread, are but loose thread"), so that the contrast between the speaker, excited about his "mummy truths" (compare the "mummy wheat" in the black centaur poem), and his supposed guest, grows sharper and their connection more dubious.

To these touches we must add the recognition that the main occasion of the poem is never fulfilled. Not only will "Yeats" never know for sure whether ghosts came, but he never gets a chance to make whatever pronouncement he has hoped the dead will listen to more seriously than the living. At the beginning of the poem we are led to expect something momentous:

> Because I have a marvellous thing to say,
> A certain marvellous thing.

This modulates in the last pair of stanzas to "I have mummy truths to tell," and to a kind of repetitive vagueness and excitement: "Such thought—such thought have I . . . Such thought, that in it bound / I need no other thing." The echo of Lear's "I will do such things" may be fortuitous or deliberate. At any rate, we never find out precisely what the "marvellous thing" and the "mummy truths" and the "such thought" consist of. The poem leaves us speculating and the speaker apparently unable to articulate his momentous insights either to the living or the dead.

When we have noted all its comic touches, its sly undercutting of Yeats's own spiritualist preoccupations, however, we do not find the poem merely ironic or deflating. The speaker's review of his dead acquaintances and imagined phantoms, as in "In Memory of Major Robert Gregory" and "The Tower," is touching and vivid. Horton is portrayed with great sympathy, Florence Emery is given a glowing tribute for her courage and wisdom, and the quarrelsomeness and lunacy of MacGregor can be overlooked:

> I thought him half a lunatic, half knave,
> And told him so, but friendship never ends;

And what if mind seem changed,
And it seem changed with the mind,
When thoughts rise up unbid
On generous things that he did
And I grow half contented to be blind.

These recognitions and reconciliations, even if only in memory, are among the rewards of old age, as portrayed in poems like "A Man Young and Old" and "Among School Children."

Moreover, the speaker comes to a further recognition when he says, having summoned three ghosts to mind, "But names are nothing. What matter who it be." As wine is nothing to wine breath, names are nothing beyond life. He welcomes any ghost. This insight relaxes the issue of who might visit, and leaves the speaker self-sufficient and exhilarated. The living would mock at his mummy truths, and the dead will not identify themselves because identity means little or nothing to them. But, instead of experiencing frustration, "Yeats" has no need for either group:

. . . such thought have I that hold it tight
Till meditation master all its part,
Nothing can stay my glance
Until that glance run in the world's despite
To where the damned have howled away their hearts,
And where the blessed dance;
Such thought, that in it bound
I need no other thing
Wound in mind's wandering,
As mummies in the mummy-cloth are wound.

The speaker's mastery, self-sufficiency, and satisfaction leave him somewhere between the living and the dead, full of sympathies and secrets, like the old man in the last three sections of "A Man Young and Old." We realize that the "certain marvellous thing" he has to say is in fact this poem, with its rich situation and complex tones, and that we have been maneuvered into a kind of neutrality where we are neither the living who would merely mock it, nor the dead who would find it inadequate or incomplete. We inhabit and appreciate the speaker's own middle ground, and when he says a second time that "maybe all that hear" what he has to say, dead and alive, "should laugh and weep an hour upon the clock," we understand the complexity of tone and ambiguity of accomplishment he has been characterizing. The limits of articulation have been reached, and the limits of knowledge have been stretched. Our main sense ought to be appreciation of the master artist who has devised poems like this one and the others in *The Tower*, poems that render the full sweep of existence, a glance that runs "in the world's despite" like Dante's, "To where the damned have howled away their hearts, / And where the blessed dance." In the absence of a supernatural structure like the one that made *The Divine Comedy* possible, Yeats has improvised in *The Tower* a series of dramatic and dramatically arranged lyrics that amount, very nearly, to the same thing.

11. A Bitter Book

In a famous exchange in Shakespeare's *Henry IV*, part 1, Glendower, the medieval Welsh warlord and mystic, boasts of his prowess as a conjuror—"I can call spirits from the vasty deep"—and Hotspur, his English guest and gadfly, responds: "Why so can I, or so can any man; / But will they come when you do call for them?" Drama by its very nature affords this kind of alternation of viewpoints, possibilities, and beliefs. Lyric poetry, on the other hand, must seek special means if it is to combine its own moments of vision, crisis, and exaltation with the energies and clashes of drama.

That Yeats was seeking such a synthesis (as he was also seeking a more lyrical kind of drama) seems clear from a careful reading of *The Tower*. That is why an account of the poems that takes their drama, their dialectic, their restless exploration of the rhythms of belief and skepticism, of confidence and despair, into consideration seems to me preferable to one that regards them simply as expressions of the poet's life or philosophy. Yeats, as the controlling artist behind *The*

Tower, draws directly on his own life and his settled and un-settled beliefs, so that we feel that his various personae and self-representations bring us closer to his life and feelings than Glendower and Hotspur bring us to Shakespeare's; but some of the same caution that we exercise about equating the views of dramatic characters with their authors is in order with a lyric design of any kind, and is essential to one as complex as *The Tower*. At the very moment when we think we have pinned down the dramatized "Yeats," his creator—master artist, conjuror, and ventriloquist—slips triumphant-ly through our grasp.

I have tried to demonstrate in the preceding chapters how Yeats presents himself to us as if he were Glendower *and* Hot-spur, confident about summoning spirits one moment and wryly doubtful the next. We need the contraries, the implicit and explicit drama, to do him justice, both as a man and as an artist. The point is that the artistic method he had fully evolved by the time of *The Tower*—a crafty mix of style, structure, and increasingly ambitious designs for volumes of poetry—needs to be understood as such and taken on its own terms if we are to fully appreciate his work as a whole.

That is not, I realize, a very fashionable emphasis. A more customary line of approach these days—I have in mind mainly deconstructionist criticism—is a demonstration of how artists fail and how language proves inadequate to their needs and aims. The problem with imposing such a view on Yeats is twofold: he seems to have been there first, anticipat-ing our sense of the problems and failures he continually faces in his attempt to make art from life and to reconcile opposites; and he seems to have slyly resolved some of the very problems we were anxious to point out in him.

At the same time, I don't wish to be accused of uncritical devotion. I may well, in the preceding pages, have overstated the case for the unity and wholeness of *The Tower*. My pursuit of its unfolding drama and my investigation of its brilliant juxtapositions have necessarily had a very positive emphasis, though not, I hope, an imprecise or single-minded one. I know that some of the juxtapositions may simply be gaps or bad seams, and no more. And I trust I have made clear that the unity I have tried to describe is not the same unity that one finds in a novel or a play, though such comparisons have often proved metaphorically useful to my speculations about the order of poems and its effect. I am content if the weight of evidence suggests that on the whole my way of reading the individual poems that make up *The Tower* makes better sense than more arbitrary ways that do not take account of the poet's methodology. My approach seems to allow the reader considerable leeway in judging just how unified the volume is and, if he or she wishes to pursue such speculation, how much its unity resembles that of literary works that are planned from the outset and generically identified as artistic wholes by precedent and by convention.

Yeats himself, of course, complicated in at least two ways the whole matter of how we should read him. One was by publishing *A Vision* in 1925, a fascinating account of a philosophical/mystical system to which he apparently gave great weight. The urge to use it as a key to his difficult poems is understandable. Even more confusing, perhaps, was his habit of using himself in his poems, a gesture that opens the door to the "romantic" reading of a poem in which the poet, spontaneously and rather helplessly, gives direct and largely unmediated utterance to his own emotions.

The double temptation to account for Yeats's ideas by *A Vision* and other such sources and to reduce the emotional meanings of the poems to details of his life has been nearly irresistible to commentators. Without repudiating its partial validity, I have tried in this study to shift the emphasis by asking the poems to speak for themselves and each other, to let Yeats's best book be its own best source of interpretation, to reveal the peculiarly modern and ingenious effect of organizing a larger whole through apparently disparate parts. Beyond the territory I have explored lies the rest of *The Collected Poems*—the plays and the essays, the autobiographical writings and the letters, and the life. A fascinating terrain, but it is not the terrain of this study. The next question of artistic wholeness involves *The Collected Poems* as an entity; my study of *The Tower* bears on that without attempting to resolve it.

I like the Glendower/Hotspur example cited above because questions of certitude and doubt, of spirits coming and not coming, seem to me crucial to the dramatized and composite representation of life and art in *The Tower*. The book is in great part a portrait of the artist as an old man. Worrying about old age, alternately questioning and reaffirming the power and value of the imagination, the central character or reigning consciousness in this book holds a complex fascination. But while the aging mage and artist whom I have called "Yeats" stands at the center, his moods alternating and his certainties mixed with uncertainties, it is the center of a large and turbulent world, stretching in many directions, spatial and temporal, a disturbing universe that both causes and reflects his ambivalence. Without its size and complexity, he might lose interest for us.

What does this brimming world include? We enter it by a backward look through time to Byzantine civilization, but soon realize that its key locale is the old Norman tower at Ballylee, near Coole, in County Galway in the west of Ireland. But from this remote location we can travel widely, both in time and space: to Athens, Babylon, Japan, and Oxford. A list of things and places Greek in this book would be especially long and impressive, but the poet's traveling glance looks on back beyond that ancient world to the prehistoric reaches of human thought where basic myths were formed, "dark night where lay / The crowns of Ninevah," the "fabulous, formless darkness" we can only guess at. As we move forward through a careful reading of *The Tower*, we learn to be equally at home in the Great Memory and in the changeable weather of the Irish countryside, in the dreaming mind of the aging artist or the majestic utterances of a Sophoclean chorus.

Birds are one prominent feature of this world. As the book begins, we encounter the birds who commend a world of change, and then the piece of golden handiwork meant to rival or displace them. Next come the swan and nesting daws of the title poem; the peacocks, moorhens, owls, starlings, and hawks of "Meditations"; and the swan's unforgettable return in "Nineteen Hundred and Nineteen." The range of bird references that stretches from Zeus as swan in the Leda sonnet to the stares, daws, and moorhens Yeats saw daily around his tower exemplifies the careful tension *The Tower* maintains between reality and myth, between ordinary experience and visionary revelation. No doubt the qualities of flight and song account for the aged speaker's attraction to birdhood in an artifice of eternity in "Sailing to Byzantium," but that same speaker, or one very like him, thinks to compare himself, as he ponders his artistic will and testament, to the chattering, screaming daws who are nesting just outside his window.

That speaker in "The Tower" determines to "make my soul," reconciling art and experience, life and death, morning and evening. We understand that the resolution is comparable to the previous poem's urge to have "Soul clap its hands and sing, and louder sing." One drama that unfolds in *The Tower*, then, is that of struggle and reconciliation, a complex pageant that finds its quiet closure in an old man "Wound in mind's wandering," aware of his limitations but determined to use meditation to master his thoughts until "Nothing can stay my glance."

What a strange procession of characters the reader encounters along the way in this pilgrimage! The ghosts of rough men-at-arms pant up and down the tower stairs and play loud dice on the tables. Mrs. French removes the cover of a dish and finds an insolent farmer's ears. A Falstaffian Irregular cracks jokes about the civil war. Loie Fuller whirls past, with floating veils. Robert Artisson, slouching, replaces her. A staring virgin tears out a living heart and carries it away, still beating, in her hand. Mary sews some purple breeches for Jesus. Leda struggles with a giant swan. Aristotle spanks his pupil, Alexander the Great. Owen Aherne converses with his own crazed heart. A mermaid drowns her lover by accident. Old Madge nurses a swaddled stone. Three public statues in Dublin break into laughter. It is a wonderful parade of human types and possibilities, drawn from every era and every walk of life.

And always, at or near the center of it, is the old man, artist and mage, whose composite self-portrait and spiritual journey we are witness to. He paces his battlements, tours a model school, tries on various guises, and sits at the end in Oxford, half-frustrated and half-satisfied, at midnight on All Soul's Night. Has he made his soul or lost it, or both? The very equivocality with which these questions must be answered becomes a part of our satisfaction and a reflection of his wisdom.

No account of *The Tower's* variety would be complete without some notice of its diction. I have stressed what Yeats achieves through simplicity, as in "I walk through the long schoolroom questioning." Other examples of that kind might include "Man is in love and loves what vanishes" and "For none alive today / Can know the stories that we know / Or say the things we say." But when we have noted how simple the diction can be, we must turn and admit how often the terms are exotic—*mummy-cloth, Quattrocento, chryselephantine, Babylonian starlight, escutcheoned doors, daemonic images, the fume of muscatel*—and how often calculatedly deflating—*fiddle-stick* and *battered kettle, juggleries, topers, crackpated,* and *scarecrows.*

It is the phrases, however, that intrigue us most, striking us with rightness and expressiveness. Some are startling—*fierce virgin, brute blood of the air, wild infancy, horrible splendour of desire, monstrous familiar images.* Others are delightful because so apt—*headlong light, slippered Contemplation, cold snows of a dream, desolate heaven, dusty wind, the mantling of the blood.* Still others seem breathtaking from their power to compress large areas of experience into compact form. "Honey of generation," for example, summons up all the pleasure, mystery, and wonder of sex and procreation. "Self-born mockers" characterizes our need for objects of worship whose perfection undermines the impulse that gave them birth. "Broken toys" makes child's play and illusion out of every serious human activity. "Galilean turbulence" evokes everything in our history that stems from the events surrounding the life and death of Jesus. "Careless muses" resonates with the frustrations inherent in the troubled relations of life and art, natural and supernatural, temporal and eternal.

These listings of images, characters, words, and phrases might go on indefinitely. I could display magical objects—a sword, a labyrinth, mummy wheat, a chestnut tree. I could show slides of "Yeats" in a great variety of postures—now pacing on his battlements, now addressing a picture, now sitting expectantly in front of two glasses of wine. I might remind the reader how the book's remarkable metonymies— "Ledaean body," "wood's intricacies," "dancer"—are really made possible by the interactions of the poems. All these activities, however, would point to the same end, a concept

surely established by now: the emotional and imaginative in-
terlocking of *The Tower*. If it is a book that makes very con-
siderable demands on its readers, it is also a book that offers
them—as I hope I have shown—very considerable rewards.
In it a poet both acknowledges his multiple cultural obliga-
tions and then partly frees himself from them by creating
a culture of his own. The new culture is a composite of
personal and impersonal, history and myth, reality and art,
elation and despair. It is uniquely modern in its multiplic-
ity and its originality, a defiant whole welded from dispar-
ate parts, a coherent world mirroring one that continually
threatens to disintegrate.

The making of the soul and the making of the book, a
single emphatic act, is a process we can follow, musically
and dramatically, by reading *The Tower* from cover to cover.
In musical terms, all the important themes are set out at
the beginning, in the magisterial and difficult opening series
that runs from "Sailing to Byzantium" to "The Tower," on to
"Meditations in Time of Civil War," and "Nineteen Hundred
and Nineteen." Old age, with its mind-body and art-reality
problems, history as destructive change and/or coherent
cycle, myth as the human imaginative response that must be
reborn as art. Art is the major theme, through the hope that
its troubled mirror can surpass other imaginative structures—
metaphysics, history, mythology—because it acknowledges
its own illusory status. By that acknowledgment it arrives at
the recognition that all the world is human fabrication, a
tragic pageant lit by the flames of our resinous hearts and
constructed "lock, stock and barrel" out of the bitter human
soul. Once the themes have been introduced, as in a great
fugue, they are elaborated and modulated in triumphant
fashion through the rest of the book, all the way to its quiet,
half-humorous, and confident close in "All Souls' Night."

If musical structure offers one analogy to the way *The*

Tower achieves unity through sequence, drama provides another. Here the invocation of Sophocles at the book's center helps us see that the old man whose portrait and pilgrimage it has become has won the same recognition that tragic dramatists confer on tragic heroes. The old man whose rage and frustration open the book ultimately validates his imagination by accepting change, by recognizing art's limitations, and by making his distress and confusion work for, rather than against, his creative impulse. He reaches a kind of plateau where he can handle difficult material like the rape of Leda that other poets would be helpless with, and where, in poems like "Among School Children," he turns loss and humiliation to triumph right before our eyes. The plateau is Sophoclean in the sense that it has a bitter and bracing air, a tingle of awful knowledge, but it is one we do not come willingly down from until, at book's end, we are released to our ordinary lives, worlds, and modes of knowledge.

Yeats himself was a little startled by what he had achieved. After he had assembled *The Tower* and seen it through the press, he sat down and reread it. He was, he wrote to Olivia Shakespear, "astonished at its bitterness." The artist who had had the fun of putting it all together was taken aback by the taste of his "full-flavoured wine." Since "bitter" is a key word in the book, pointing again and again to the basic tragedy of the human condition, we can understand Yeats's comment as expressing surprise at how clearly the tragic vision came through. Certainly he understood how that bitter flavor was bound up with the extent of his accomplishment: "that bitterness gave the book its power and it is the best book I have written."[36] One can also add that the bitter is only one of many flavors here, and no more the whole truth of the volume than if Yeats had found some other attribute dominant. The bitterness, to my way of thinking, moderates as the book goes forward, being strongest in "Nineteen Hundred and

Nineteen" and more tranquil in the second half. A tragic vi-
sion of life certainly underlies the volume as a whole, but in
its triumphant art and its ways of affirming the strength of
the imagination, especially in the face of old age and histori-
cal adversity, *The Tower* undercuts its own pessimism by its
celebration of the human capacity for making: making up
"the whole," making myths and prayers and poems and songs
and arguments and lullabies. Making a soul, and making a
book of poems as fine and unified as *The Tower*.

Finally, we might glance once more at the issue of modern-
ism. I noted at the beginning of this study that Yeats's relation
to modernism in the arts was problematic. If we take him at
his word, or at his most opinionated and cranky (as, for ex-
ample, in assembling *The Oxford Book of Modern Verse*), we
might well conclude that Yeats was stuck fast in some com-
bination of Celtic twilight and Pre-Raphaelite glamor. And
there is certainly no point in pretending that he was inspired,
in writing *The Tower*, by cubism or by the dadaist move-
ment.[37] But the book itself belies the criticism that Yeats's
practice scarcely took him beyond the ideas about art that
were current at the time of Ruskin and Pater. Yeats may have
been more modern, and more modernist, than he knew or
cared to let on. Perhaps the "bitterness" that astonished him
a little was the flavor of innovation. There simply had never
been a book of lyric poems that created unity out of multi-
plicity and fragmentation in the way that *The Tower* did. We
cannot speak of modernism in lyric poetry simply by cit-
ing the work of more avowed modernists like Williams and
Pound (to limit the question to poetry in English for the mo-
ment), for in doing so we overlook the originality and inno-
vation of Yeats's later work. We now have sufficient perspec-
tive on some of the modernist literary masterpieces—I would
cite Mandelstam's and Montale's poetry, Rilke's *Duino Elegies*,
and Eliot's *The Waste Land* as other significant examples—to

understand that they were trying to preserve and even renew a significant connection to an older world and a heritage that stretched back to the beginnings of Western culture. The effort was not a retreat from their modernism but a significant part of it.

Surely that is what we need to recognize about Yeats. *The Tower* is enormously innovative in the way it involves the reader, acknowledges a world that is shattered and chaotic, and insists on the right to create new literary forms and redefine traditional notions of unity. But it is also, like Pound's *Cantos* or Eliot's *Four Quartets*, an attempt to rival poets like Dante and Milton. Toward the close of "All Souls' Night" Yeats speaks of using "meditation" to master experience and thought in such a way that

> Nothing can stay my glance
> Until that glance run in the world's despite
> To where the damned have howled away their hearts,
> And where the blessed dance.

That is a Dantesque ambition, but its realization takes a modern, rather than a Romantic or a Victorian form—daring, equivocal, even contradictory; a glance that runs "in the world's despite" both accepts modern reality and refuses to be beaten by it. Whether Yeats knew it or not, he was keeping company with the best that was being accomplished in the modernist era. Far from being an unwilling participant in the great artistic changes of this century, he was a leader who showed the way.

Notes

1. "The Sacred Book of Arts," in *Gnomon* (New York: McDowell Obolensky, 1958), p. 14. This crucial essay is also collected in *Yeats: A Collection of Critical Essays*, ed. John Unterecker, Twentieth Century Views (Englewood, N.J.: Prentice-Hall, 1963), pp. 10–22. See also Thomas Parkinson, *W. B. Yeats: The Later Poetry* (Berkeley: University of California Press, 1966), pp. 55–57.
2. This information is drawn from *The Variorum Edition of the Poems of W. B. Yeats*, ed. Peter Allt and Russell K. Alspach (New York: Macmillan, 1957).
3. See Curtis Bradford, "Yeats's Byzantium Poems: A Study of Their Development," in Unterecker, *Yeats*, pp. 93–130.
4. Noted by Kenner, p. 28, and in the discussion of this poem that forms a considerable part of the first chapter of Daniel Albright's *The Myth Against Myth: A Study of Yeats's Imagination in Old Age* (London: Oxford University Press, 1972).
5. I am indebted to David Walker for several of the ideas in this discussion of "The Tower."
6. Other poems in the volume that include dates are "Youth and Age" (1924), "Leda and the Swan" (1923), "The Gift of Harun

Al-Rashid" (1923), and "All Souls' Night" (1920). The date on the last of these was not included in the first edition.

7. W. B. Yeats, *A Vision* (New York: Macmillan, 1961), p. 268.

8. As discussed in his essay "The Noble Rider and the Sound of Words," in *The Necessary Angel* (New York: Knopf, 1951).

9. Thomas R. Whitaker, *Swan and Shadow: Yeats's Dialogue with History* (Chapel Hill: University of North Carolina Press, 1964), p. 178.

10. Yeats's own note is useful here: "I suppose that I must have put hawks into the fourth stanza because I have a ring with a hawk and a butterfly on it, to symbolize the straight road of logic, and so of mechanism, and the crooked road of intuition: 'For wisdom is a butterfly and not a gloomy bird of prey.'"

11. The phrase is from "In Memory of Eva Gore-Booth and Con Markiewicz," in *The Winding Stair and Other Poems*: "We the great gazebo built, / They convicted us of guilt."

12. Whitaker, *Swan and Shadow*, p. 230.

13. Yeats's sense of "play" seems to include sex and frivolity, but he often connects it with reductive attitudes toward art. See my discussion of the sequence "Upon a Dying Lady" in "The Living World for Text: Life and Art in *The Wild Swans at Coole*," in *The Author in His Work*, ed. Louis Martz and Aubrey Williams (New Haven: Yale University Press, 1978), pp. 148–49.

14. Whitaker, *Swan and Shadow*, p. 230.

15. We come here to one of the few "seams" in *The Tower*. Originally, the poem "Wisdom" appeared after the earlier version of "Two Songs from a Play." By 1933, when he was assembling *Collected Poems*, Yeats had not only written the additional stanza for "Two Songs," but "Fragments." He put the latter in "Wisdom"'s place, moving "Wisdom" deeper into the volume, to follow "Colonus' Praise." The two-volume edition of 1949 brings "Wisdom" back to a place between "Fragments" and "Leda and the Swan," but that does not necessarily reflect Yeats's preference, as Richard J. Finneran's recent *Editing Yeats's Poems* (London: Macmillan, 1983) shows. Finneran's own new edition, *The Poems of W. B. Yeats: A New Edition* (London and New York: Macmillan, 1983), retains the 1933 placement of "Wisdom," as

Fig. 2. Watercolor by Edmund Dulac for Hawthorne's *Tanglewood Tales*, 1918. The caption reads, "The good Chiron taught his pupils how to play upon the harp." 12 x 11 in.

opposed to 1949. Rather than try to argue that one or the other represents Yeats's most considered or final judgment, I will simply contend here that the earlier placement of "Wisdom" reflects my own preference, and that is why I discuss it out of the sequence in which readers will find it in the standard *Collected Poems* (1956) or in Finneran's new edition. My text for the additions to *The Tower* is Finneran's new edition.

16. Yvor Winters, *The Poetry of W. B. Yeats* (Denver: A. Swallow, 1960), p. 8.

17. Harold Bloom, *Yeats* (New York: Oxford University Press, 1970), pp. 364–65.

18. Robert Snukal, *High Talk: The Philosophical Poetry of W. B. Yeats* (Cambridge: Cambridge University Press, 1973), pp. 167–68.

19. Ibid., p. 168.

20. Joseph Hone, *W. B. Yeats* (New York: Macmillan, 1943), pp. 348–50.

21. For an account of Yeats's commissions and examples of Dulac's centaurs, see Colin White, *Edmund Dulac* (New York: Scribner's, 1976), pp. 92–97. A typical Dulac centaur from the illustrations to *Tanglewood Tales* is included as figure 2.

22. Hone, *W. B. Yeats*, p. 349.

23. See my discussion of "In Memory of Major Robert Gregory" in "The Living World for Text," pp. 144–46.

24. In his note at the end of *The Tower* Yeats uses quotation marks, as if to leave open to question just what the source of the material is: "I have taken the 'honey of generation' from Porphyry's essay on 'The Cave of the Nymphs' but find no warrant in Porphyry for considering it the 'drug' that destroys the 'recollection' of pre-natal freedom."

25. John Unterecker, in *A Reader's Guide to William Butler Yeats* (New York: Noonday Press, 1959), discusses parallels between "Colonus' Praise" and "Among School Children," as does Kenner in "The Sacred Book of the Arts."

26. Peter Ure, *W. B. Yeats* (Edinburgh: Oliver and Boyd, 1963), speaks of "A Man Young and Old," along with "A Woman Young and Old" and "Words for Music Perhaps," as being set in "a

Fig. 3. Gouache by Sir Edward Burne-Jones, "The Depths of the Sea," 1887. 77 x 30 in., the Fogg Art Gallery, Cambridge, Mass. This is a copy of an 1886 painting, now in Australia.

naked world which has the final discipline and stylisation of a very bare playing-place. It is a huge, sparse world with a few prototypical characters" (p. 80).

27. See Finneran, *Poems*, p. 700.

28. Unterecker, *Reader's Guide*, p. 194.

29. This exquisite six-line poem seems to be based on the late Burne-Jones painting "The Depths of the Sea" (1887), of which three versions exist. See Martin Harrison and Bill Walters, *Burne-Jones* (London: Putnam, 1973), p. 142 (illustrated in figure 3).

30. See A. Norman Jeffares, *W. B. Yeats: Man and Poet* (London: Routledge and Kegan Paul, 1949), p. 244.

31. *The Letters of W. B. Yeats*, ed. Allan Wade (London: R. Hart Davis, 1954), pp. 840–41.

32. The second line of this lyric in the first edition of *The Tower* has "their" for "there."

33. The phrase is Unterecker's (*Reader's Guide*, p. 197).

34. Richard Ellmann, *The Identity of Yeats* (New York: Oxford University Press, 1964), p. 174.

35. In the first edition of *The Tower* Yeats identifies Horton only by an initial: "H——'s the first I call."

36. Wade, *Letters*, p. 742.

37. Parkinson, in *W. B. Yeats: The Later Poetry*, gives an excellent summary of Yeats's reactions to modernism, especially as espoused by Pound, in his chapter "The Embodiment of Truth" (pp. 1–72). While my conclusions about Yeats's significant relation to modernism are somewhat different, I found his account extremely helpful.

Index

"All Souls' Night," 126–133, 141
"Among School Children," 80, 85–96, 99–102, 107–108, 112, 116, 119, 124, 127–128, 132, 142, 148

Ballylee, 12, 31, 127
Bloom, Harold, 76–77
Byzantium, 15–16

"The Cold Heaven," 56
"Colonus' Praise," 97–103, 148

Dante, 5, 133, 144
"Deconstructionist" readings, xi, 19–20, 135
Design of The Tower, xii–xiv
Diction, 21, 67, 139–140

Dramatic oppositions, xi, 4, 134–135
Dulac, Edmund, 82, 147–148

Eliot, T. S., 40
Emery, Florence, 129

Finneran, Richard, xii, 146, 150
First edition of The Tower, xii–xiv
First experiments with order and sequence, 11–13
"The Fisherman," 8
"The Fool by the Roadside," 103–104, 130
"Fragments," 70–71, 75, 99–100, 104, 138
Fuller, Loie, 47, 51, 58, 66, 100, 106

"The Gift of Harun Al-Rashid,"
13, 117, 121–125
Gonne, Iseult, 104, 106, 113
Gonne, Maud, 24, 89, 93

Humanism, 26–27

"In Memory of Major Robert
Gregory," 148
Intertextuality, xi, 5

Joyce, James, 2–3
Juxtaposition, xi, 6–11

Kenner, Hugh, v, 5–6, 145, 148

"Leda and the Swan," 73–78, 80,
83, 138

"A Man Young and Old," 103,
107–119, 128, 132–133, 148
"Meditations in Time of Civil
War," 30–45, 48, 49–50, 56,
62, 64, 67, 91, 100, 107–108,
117, 119, 122, 124, 138, 141
Montessori, Maria, 87
Moore, T. Sturge, xii

"The New Faces," 61–62
"Nineteen Hundred and Nine-
teen," 46–60, 65, 69, 91, 99,
101, 108, 112, 121, 130, 138, 141–
143

Oedipus, 98–99
Oedipus at Colonus, 79, 97–103,
105, 117, 119

Old age, 16–18, 20, 62, 86, 98,
105, 114–116, 118–119, 121, 137,
139
"On a Picture of a Black Cen-
taur by Edmund Dulac," 78–
84, 86, 100, 130
Ottava rima, 14–15, 86
"Owen Aherne and his Danc-
ers," 104–106, 108, 112

Parkinson, Thomas, 145, 150
Plato and Platonists, 53, 92
"A Prayer for My Daughter,"
9–10, 62
"A Prayer for My Son," 62–64,
75, 91

Rackham, Arthur, 82

"Sailing to Byzantium," xi, 14–
20, 83, 86, 117, 119, 124, 138,
141
Salkeld, Cecil, 82–83
"The Second Coming," 9–10,
56, 67
Sequences as models of The
Tower, 32, 107–108, 119
Shakespearean analogues, 23,
104, 131, 133
Snukal, Robert, 77–78
Sophocles, 98–99
Spenser, Edmund, ix, 2
Stevens, Wallace, 39
Symbolist aesthetic, 16, 46, 51,
74

"The Three Monuments," 117, 120–122
"The Tower," xi, 7, 20–29, 69, 86, 91, 108, 112, 128, 131, 138, 141
"Two Songs from a Play," 65–71, 75, 91, 104

"Upon a Dying Lady," 146
Ure, Peter, v

"The Valley of the Black Pig," 56
A Vision, 126, 136

Walker, David, xiv, 145
"The Wheel," 61–62, 69, 104, 117

Whitaker, T. R., 41, 57, 146
Wilde, Oscar, 2, 55, 58
Winters, Yvor, 76–77
"Wisdom," 71–72, 75, 91
Wordsworth, William, ix, 5, 21

Yeats: and the English poetic tradition, 1–2, 14, 74, 86; cultural allegiances, x, 1–4, 31, 86, 127; modernity and relation to international modernism, ix–x, 2–3, 5, 74, 86–87, 143–144; uses of metonymy, 67, 75
"Youth and Age," 61–62